HYPOCHONDRIA

What's Behind the
Hidden Costs
of Healthcare in America

Hal Rosenbluth and Marnie Hall

RODIN
BOOKS.

Hardcover ISBN 978-1-957588-28-5
eBook ISBN 978-1-957588-29-2

PUBLISHED BY RODIN BOOKS INC
666 Old Country Road
Suite 510
Garden City, New York 11530
www.rodinbooks.com

Book and cover design by Barbara Aronica

Manufactured in the United States of America

DISCLAIMER

This book contains the opinions and ideas of its authors. The book describes the authors' personal experience and provides information on the subjects discussed. The authors and publisher are not engaged in rendering medical, health, or any other kind of personal or professional services in the book. Readers are advised to consult with healthcare professionals about all matters pertaining to their health and well-being. The authors and publisher specifically disclaim all responsibility for any liability, loss, or risk, personal or otherwise, which is incurred as a consequence, directly or indirectly, of the use and application of any of the contents of this book.

In appreciation of Matthew J. Killion, MD,
America's finest internist

CONTENTS

INTRODUCTION

Halloween should have been fun. My friend Stan's family had joined ours to traipse through a nearby neighborhood with our children to celebrate. Jack-o'-lanterns grinned on porch steps and paper ghosts rustled in the trees. Tiny goblins, witches, princesses, and superheroes roamed the sidewalks, shrieking and giggling.

Then, halfway through the evening, my lungs suddenly seized up. My breathing turned ragged. In seconds, my heart was galloping in my chest and sweat was raining down my forehead. My legs threatened to collapse with fatigue.

This is it, I thought. *I'm going to die.*

I'd recently returned from Washington, DC. Since taking over Rosenbluth International, my family's travel company, I'd grown it from a $20 million local travel agency in Philadelphia to a $6 billion global travel management company in thirty-five countries through innovation and superior service. In the wake of the harrowing 9/11 terrorist attacks, I'd been called to testify before Congress about the impact of terrorism on the travel industry. I'd also personally spoken with various senators in preparation for my testimony and had visited Senate Majority Leader

Tom Daschle's office, which I soon learned had received an envelope containing anthrax spores. So far, the anthrax attacks had killed five people and injured seventeen others in the two weeks following my visit.

Now, on Halloween 2001, it came to me in a blinding flash that I would be the next anthrax victim. Senator Daschle was one of the first to receive a letter laced with anthrax and *I had been in his office that same day.*

As a news junkie, I'd memorized the symptoms of anthrax poisoning listed by the Centers for Disease Control (CDC): fever and chills, shortness of breath, chest pains, headache, sweats, extreme fatigue, body aches.

Check, check, check: Yes, I had every one of those symptoms! I must have inhaled anthrax. Death was lurking around the corner, a ghoul in a black shroud.

Stan, our wives, and the children reached another house. The kids rang the bell. "Trick or treat!" they cried when the door opened.

A minute later, I heard my daughter say, "Wait, where's Dad?"

I had lagged behind and was now rushing to the car, clutching my chest and race-walking on wobbly legs. Would I make it to the hospital in time?

"Where are you going, Hal?" Stan yelled.

"To the emergency room," I called without turning around. "I think I have anthrax poisoning!"

"Oh my God," said my wife, Renee. "There he goes again. Hal probably just wants to get out of another Halloween loop around the neighborhood."

At the emergency room, the nurses asked me a few questions and checked my vitals. Then they kicked me to the curb and suggested I head home and see which treats I wanted to ingest.

Stan called me the next day. "Well? What's the verdict? How are you?"

"I don't have anthrax."

He laughed. "No kidding. The thing about you, Hal, is that you're sticky, like flypaper. Every disease you hear about sticks to you."

In some part of my mind, I had known I didn't have anthrax even as I floored the accelerator to drive to the hospital in record time. But, if you're a hypochondriac like me (or, as it's listed in the *Diagnostic and Statistical Manual of Mental Disorders*, someone with "somatic symptom disorder" or "illness anxiety disorder"), fact and fiction are equal. Your symptoms are *real*. And, with the help of a little doom scrolling online, they add up to a terminal illness. When I was diagnosed as having type 2 diabetes in my forties, for instance, I went straight from monitoring my sugar levels to imagining my limbs being amputated. Or at least my toes.

For a hypochondriac, that severe pain in your back

signals kidney cancer. Your headache after mowing the lawn on a hot day? That can't possibly be dehydration. It must be the telltale forewarning symptom of a brain tumor with a seizure.

I consider myself a "cognizant" hypochondriac, which means I am fully aware of this collision of fact and fiction in my own mind. I know I probably don't have whatever I think I have. Yet, I keep my doctor on speed dial anyhow, because *you never know.*

• • •

Sometimes I wish there were AA sorts of meetings I could attend, safe spaces where I could stand up in front of people and confess: "Hi, I'm Hal, and I'm a hypochondriac."

Since I can't do that, I'm writing this book.

My intent is to share my journey through the healthcare system as a hypochondriac, an odyssey that, *in the past two years alone*, has resulted in 39 medical claims, 210 prescription claims, and countless medical tests, including a full-body scan and an extensive blood panel test that would have made former Theranos CEO Elizabeth Holmes jealous. Together, my coauthor, Marnie Hall, and I will shed light on the overall impact hypochondria can have on individuals whose relationships and careers suffer when illness anxiety rules our lives.

Almost everyone worries about getting sick or dying. Anxiety about our health can be a good thing, because it makes us more attentive to symptoms and keeps us going to the doctor for routine check-ups and medical tests.

However, people with hypochondria take that anxiety to the next level, living in dread that every small ache signals the Beginning of the End. We take up more than our share of visits to doctors, clinics, and hospitals. We also spend an inordinate amount of time searching for health information online, feeling distressed by our search results, and seeking multiple opinions when we don't like the answer one provider gives us.

The end result is that those who suffer from illness anxiety end up costing an already costly healthcare system a great deal of money. According to a 2023 report by the Peter G. Peterson Foundation, the United States has one of the most expensive healthcare systems in the world.[1] In 2021, the U.S. spent a whopping $4.3 trillion on healthcare, or about $12,900 per person. "By comparison," the report authors add, "the average cost of healthcare per person in other wealthy countries is only about half as much." What's even more worrying is that "relative to the size of the economy, healthcare costs have increased over the past few decades, from 5 percent of GDP in 1960 to 18 percent in 2021."[2]

An analysis published in *Third Way* in 2023 reports that "10 million working-age Americans have families that spend more than 5% of their household income on medical bills for two years in a row. When paired with costs of insurance, health care is taking a total of 14% to 15% of their income."[3]

Why are Americans taking such a huge hit on healthcare?

There are several underlying factors. The biggest is something we can't do anything about: the U.S. population is getting older. According to the U.S. Census Bureau's July 2022 estimate, 17.3 percent of Americans were over sixty-five, and it's inevitable that more of us will need more healthcare as we age.[4]

Beyond that, we can point to our new healthcare technologies, which lead to better but more expensive procedures; hospital consolidations, which give providers the chance to increase prices; and the administrative waste involved in our complex system of insurance and provider payments.

How do people with illness anxiety impact those costs? There isn't a lot of research available on that topic, largely because most hypos like me either don't recognize that they're worrying an excessive amount about their health or don't want to admit it. But research suggests that "hypochondria accounts for at least 5 percent of all general medicine consultations in the United States," and that people with illness anxiety "can have medical costs 10 times higher than the national average."[5] In turn, that is increasing the cost for all Americans, because premiums, co-pays, and self-insured companies are the recipients of the increased cost burden.

In addition to revealing the hidden impact of hypochondria on our country's already overburdened healthcare system and provoking a conversation about what can be done to alleviate that, we'll also highlight the many ways in which our healthcare system is in need of repair and reimagining. The United States spends three and four times more than other high-income countries, such as Japan and New Zealand, but has the lowest life expectancy at birth and highest death rates for treatable conditions.[6] Health outcomes in the United States rank closer to countries with the worst health outcomes, such as Latvia and Turkey, which have bottom-of-the-barrel statistics when it comes to life expectancy after birth and managing diabetes.[7]

Thinking about Latvia makes me recall the time I traveled there with my wife. We were on a relaxing cruise, or so I thought, stopping at various Balkan ports daily with extensive shore excursions. When we reached Latvia, I stuffed my face at the breakfast buffet while dreading the imminent shore excursion.

After walking around the capital and seeing the same kinds of things we had seen the day before at a previous stop, Renee insisted that we take a train and visit the sites of another bland gray town to make the most of our day. By that point, I had simply lost all my strength and needed to bail out of the next walking tour that lay beyond the upcoming train ride, so I begged for forgiveness and headed back to the port terminal.

By the time Renee returned to the cruise ship, all of my symptoms were gone, and I was in the pool sipping on a fruity cocktail with an umbrella on top. Was it that I didn't want to see another Baltic town square, or was I truly about to faint? In retrospect, probably both things were true.

My own illness anxiety has led me to make frequent trips to doctor's offices, clinics, and hospitals. I'll share some of those anecdotes in this book and describe how my experiences have led me to reach some shocking conclusions about how inadequately, and sometimes inappropriately, so many American people are served by our healthcare system. In addition to analyzing just how much people with illness anxiety are costing the healthcare system, we'll highlight many of the issues with that system, discussing how they came to be and offering practical, easy-to-implement solutions—one of which is to curb the costly overuse of our healthcare system by people like me.

· · ·

I'm intimately familiar with the U.S. healthcare system not only as a patient (albeit often with nothing acutely wrong with me), but also as a professional who has spent decades analyzing our country's healthcare system and trying to improve it.

How did I get to this place in my career? When I sold my global travel management company, Rosenbluth International, to American Express in 2003, I was looking for my Next Big Thing. Part of my search involved creating a home office and establishing my own news monitoring system by setting up seven computer screens around the room. Placing myself in the middle of this fishbowl of information, I watched world news and read periodicals around the clock. For weeks I sat marinating in media, waiting for the most prevalent themes and ideas to bubble up to the top. My goal was to discover an *unknown, unmet need* I could solve that would make the world a better place. I had already started one new industry and was looking to create another to help improve people's lives. This can only happen if you think about it first.

If this goal sounds too altruistic to be true, bear in mind that my family's philanthropic roots reach far back in time. I want to honor that legacy. In 1892, my great-grandfather Marcus Rosenbluth, a Hungarian immigrant, founded Rosenbluth Travel when he began selling steamship tickets from his Philadelphia neighborhood. For $25 (which would be about $845 in 2022 dollars), he provided steamship passage from Eastern European ports to New York, helped passengers enter the U.S., and arranged transportation for them from Ellis Island to Philadelphia. Marcus spoke nine languages and acted as a family advisor to his clients, many of whom gave him nickels and dimes to put in savings accounts until they had enough money to bring more family members to the New World.

My own father, Harold, was equally philanthropic. He served in U.S. general George S. Patton's army during World War II and was always a generous patron to the arts. He was also deeply committed not only to Judaism, but to all faiths. He was president of Congregation Rodeph Shalom from 1976 to 1980 and a member of the board of the Institute for Jewish-Catholic relations at Saint Joseph's University in Philadelphia, where he helped fund a statue to honor the help Catholics provided to Jews during the Holocaust. He was even visited and blessed by the Pope when he went to Philadelphia. He also regularly invited young musicians from the Curtis Institute of Music, a private conservatory, to play in our home so his friends could experience their music and the artists could develop greater confidence in their performances.

Following in the footsteps of my father and grandfather, I worked hard to create a positive environment for my employees as I built Rosenbluth International into a global travel company. We earned acclaim as one of the "Hundred Best Companies to Work for in America" from *Fortune Magazine*. I even wrote a *New York Times* best-selling book called *The Customer Comes Second*, spelling out how to create a great service organization by focusing on your colleagues first and removing all the normal corporate and emotional impediments so they could concentrate solely on our clients' needs. I had even hired an in-house psychologist so that anyone at the company could talk to about professional or personal problems; the company simply received a monthly invoice with nothing on it but the amount due.

• • •

Occasionally my wife, Renee, would poke her head into my dark cocoon of computer screens and news sources. "What are you doing in here, Hal?" she'd ask.

"Working."

"No, you're not. You're just staring into space. At least come out and get some air, for God's sake."

"I just have to wait here," I'd counter. "Something will come to me."

And it did, albeit months later.

At that time, Massachusetts had become the first state to provide universal healthcare coverage. The upshot was chaos: in Massachusetts, it was nearly impossible to get a doctor, and it might take weeks to book an appointment if you were lucky enough to obtain one. It dawned on me that this might become commonplace in the future, and that we'd have a country devoid of the number of healthcare providers required to treat ill people seeking help.

This event happened to coincide with my idea to send a film crew over to Washington Square Park in Philadelphia. "Take your camera and talk with as many people as you can," I instructed. "Ask them what they hope and pray for when they close their eyes at night."

To my amazement, when I reviewed the film footage, every response was the same: those people in the park all said that the one thing they prayed for above everything else was the health and well-being of their family and friends.

My goal crystallized in that instant: the thing I could do to make the biggest difference in people's lives was to offer them affordable, high-quality, accessible, equitable healthcare.

As I was mulling over how to do this, I fell into conversation one day with Peter Miller, my then eleven-year-old son's soccer coach, who also happened to be the youngest president of Johnson & Johnson's Janssen pharmaceutical division.

"What are you doing these days, Hal?" Peter asked after one gruelingly comical practice, where nearly every kid fell or collided with something or someone, leaving most out on injury.

"Not much, really," I said.

"Maybe we should do something together," Peter suggested.

I laughed. "You're the youngest president of one of J&J's pharmaceutical companies. Why would you want to do something with me?"

"Let's just think about it. I bet we could come up with something fun."

I had always admired Peter's ability to take a bunch of *Bad News Bears* eleven-year-olds who played like they were at a piñata party, teach them self-esteem, and turn them into a winning team. That was enough for me to want to partner with him.

Peter and I spent a few weeks kicking things around and laughing our butts off about everything and nothing until we hit on an idea we liked: Why not create clinics in pharmacies nationwide, places where people in every kind of neighborhood could get their basic healthcare needs met for the lowest possible cost not only to them, but to insurers, the uninsured, and employers, too?

To that end, in 2004 we created Take Care Health Systems, a nationwide pharmacy clinic business with single-source national contracts with Walgreens, Rite-Aid, Osco-Savon, and Eckerd Drugs. I continued using my "customers come second" philosophy and structured the company to foster a corporate culture that would keep my employees happy and healthy.

The company was a huge success. We were able to employ new technologies and services to help give people access to care for as much as 80 percent less than an emergency room visit and 30–40 percent less than at their doctor's office.

In 2007, Walgreens bought us out and I became senior executive officer and president of Walgreens Co. and president of the company's Health and Wellness division. In this role I was responsible for the largest share of $63 billion in annual company revenue and contracts with health plans, health systems, government agencies, employers, pharmacy benefit manager companies (PBMs), corporate consulting firms, thousands of clinics, on-campus care centers, and over 2,500 providers of all levels.

After five years, I moved on from that position. I was bored and itched to find a new project—something else that could make a big difference in people's lives. As with my previous businesses, I wanted this new endeavor to fall within the intersection of health, culture, well-being, and technology. The result is my current venture, New Ocean Health Solutions, a dynamic software company focused exclusively on solutions for the healthcare ecosystem.

There continues to be a shortage of providers, and we can expect that to get worse in the United States. New Ocean Health provides information and activities to people between visits to their providers, helping patients manage chronic conditions and improve their overall health on a personalized basis, not one-size-fits-all. Our overall business goal is to improve health outcomes and reduce costs of care through a mobile-first enterprise integration platform that includes a fully customized digital suite of personalized programs for employers, their employees, health plans, and health systems.

Basically, what we want for every one of our clients and their employees is to replicate the healthy, vibrant culture we had created at Rosenbluth International, carried through to Take Care Health Systems where we tried to develop a culture that challenged Walgreens by delivering inspirational leadership and coaching to foster open communication to increase workforce productivity and positivity. Our end game was always the same: to maximize health and well-being for customers while maximizing that company's profit.

When I add up the many years I've spent analyzing and building better healthcare resources, the number is mind-boggling. But here's the irony: I'm still a hypochondriac who has my doctor on speed dial. In addition to having a multitude of visits to doctor's offices and emergency rooms and having batteries of unnecessary medical tests every year, I keep a blood pressure monitor, a smart scale, and a pulse oximeter in my office. I believe, on an embarrassingly regular basis, that I am having a heart attack/kidney stones/migraines/pancreatic cancer.

Often, I am in complete distress until I actually get to

an emergency room, where I'm soothed by the idea that the white coats will save me from whatever impending doom has entered my brain.

My coauthor, Marnie, sees things differently.

As a mother to four children, Marnie is of course no stranger to doctor's offices or the emergency room, either. "After all, doesn't every new parent find themselves awakened by their infant's bloodcurdling screams at some point," she says, "followed by a heart-thumping call to the after-hours nurse, which, after fifteen minutes of interrogation, ends with a flat 'Can you come to the emergency department now?'"

With each of her children, Marnie has had to handle new healthcare crises, from infant ear infections and fevers to Rollerblade ankle sprains, stitches in the forehead, big toe infections after fishing in the creek, one incident of swallowing aluminum foil, and an earring stuck sideways through an eleven-year-old girl's ear. For the most part (except for the aluminum foil), all the incidents warranted treatment. No imaginary illness or panic driven symptoms involved.

When it comes to health, Marnie has learned that information is everything. "If I have made it to the emergency room, I have entered what I call my complete freak-out zone," she says. "Medicine scares me. The idea of knowing there is something wrong with me sends me to my

Catholic knees praying to God for mercy on my soul and, yes, on my body."

Marnie's first line of treatment for health crises is "wait and see." The second line of treatment is over-the-counter medicine "and advice from my mother, or maybe the pharmacist."

Her very last possible alternative is to see a provider. "And in between all of those decisions, I am Googling, researching, and finding at-home treatments," she says.

Marnie claims she wasn't always this astute about health, mainly because she's a healthy person who doesn't have any chronic conditions. She works out regularly, eats right, prays, and meditates. She is much more afraid of her children getting sick than she fears her own health going downhill.

In other words, my coauthor is the opposite of a hypochondriac. She does worry about her health, like anyone does, but in a very different way than I do.

"In general, when it comes to my own health, doctors—with their offices, forms, questions, and labs—both frustrate and scare the living hell out of me," she says. "I think part of it has to do with loving my children so much that I worry about them having something wrong. Or, I worry that I will die, and lament the thought that they might have to go through life without me. Every well-woman visit or yearly exam opens up that 'What if?' question."

She recognizes this is a normal sort of worrying, however, and a far cry from my frequent-flyer status as a healthcare consumer.

Befitting her career as a journalist and TV producer, Marnie is skilled in researching the heck out of a subject. She has done that with our book, which, if you're reading it, means you're likely either a hypochondriac yourself, or know someone who is.

Or maybe you chose to read this book because you're a healthcare professional, insurer, or a human resources or benefits manager interested in examining the overall healthcare system in this country to improve it or utilize the best parts of it. In any case, I hope my personal journey through the U.S. healthcare ecosystem, along with Marnie's research abilities and no-nonsense views on the current state and future of healthcare, will make the topic of illness anxiety disorder relatable, informative, and even entertaining.

My hope is that by combining our own expertise with that of a broad range of research on all aspects of healthcare, we'll shed light on the issue of hypochondria in the broader social context of today's American culture. Whether you're a healthcare executive, medical practitioner, someone who works in healthcare insurance, or a patient trying to navigate the unholy maze of co-pays and healthcare bills, you'll find some eye-popping information here. This is especially true in the aftermath of COVID-19 and everything the pandemic revealed about the condition of our healthcare system—creaky, crippled, and just plain broken in places—especially when it comes to long-standing systemic problems including access barriers, outlandish costs, and widespread inequities in healthcare. And, with the ever-increasing presence of depression and anxiety in this country, these problems will inevitably get worse.

By uncovering the hidden costs of hypochondria, Marnie and I hope to spark a national conversation that leads to serious cost-cutting measures and wider access to the increasing availability of quality healthcare practices and technologies that offer digital therapeutics and holistic care. Most important, we hope to influence a cultural shift in the approach America takes toward health, with the happy result of decreased costs for all Americans and the healthcare ecosystem in general. At the same time, our goal is to help hypochondriacs recognize that they're not nuts, and that they can take steps to make life more enjoyable for themselves and the people who love them.

CHAPTER ONE

The More I Watched, the Sicker I Got

News junkies like me are suckers for punishment. We constantly watch the news on TV and follow the headlines on our phones and computers, soaking up the many horrors of the world.

A few years ago, I realized that the more news I watched, the more concerned I became, to the point at which I couldn't fall asleep at night. Or, if I did, I'd wake up in the middle of the night, anxiety-ridden and breathless with too many thoughts competing for attention. It was as if a giant dog was sitting on my chest, making it impossible to breathe. I began every morning filled with dread, my nerves jangled from lack of sleep, my shoulders knotted with tension, all of which I kept hidden from my family.

Finally, I discussed my anxiety and insomnia with my physician, who prescribed an anti-anxiety medication. Voila! The sleeplessness and constant worrying receded after taking this miracle drug. I was a new man.

Everything went well until I started worrying that my memory was slipping and decided to look into the side effects of my anti-anxiety drug online. To my utter alarm, memory loss was one of the key side effects listed for this particular medication. I leapt into action and began surveying family members.

"Is my memory slipping?" I asked my wife.

"Yes, and I've been noticing it for some time now," Renee answered with a grin. "Remember how we talked about our honeymoon, and you couldn't even remember the places we went?"

I thought back to that conversation and felt oddly better about forgetting some details. It was the drug. I had an excuse!

Still, just to be sure, I asked one of my sons if he'd noticed anything. "Do you think I'm more forgetful than I used to be?"

He answered my question with one of his own: "Isn't that why you take medicine for ADHD, Dad?"

Oh, right. I was taking so many pills; I'd nearly forgotten about that one. Why did I forget about it? Was memory loss a side effect of my anti-anxiety drug, or part of my ADHD? Or did this mean the ADHD medicine wasn't working? Another thought: Did I actually have ADHD in the first place?

Next, I approached my daughter, Jessica, who's an athlete and one of the healthiest people I know. "Jessica, do I forget stuff?"

"If you're feeling forgetful, Dad, you need better

nutrition and more exercise," she said at once. "You need to change your diet. I've told you about that before, you know. But maybe you forgot."

Jessica proceeded to send me a list of supplements and began calling me almost daily to ask if I was okay. Sometimes I didn't answer her calls because I was too busy reading the potential side effects of my new supplements and never wanted her to worry.

Given the dire results of this little research project, I now felt supremely confident that my memory was on its last legs. There was no solution other than the obvious: I should stop taking my anti-anxiety drug immediately.

I called my doctor at that time and announced my decision.

"Well, Hal, you're going to need to withdraw slowly," he advised. "I'd suggest you do it under my supervision over a period of weeks, or even months."

Unfortunately, he was going on vacation. I wasn't about to wait. The next day, I cut my dosage in half.

During this same time frame, I became enamored of a new drug for diabetes. I was first diagnosed with type 2 diabetes in my forties. I'd been flying all over the world for work, which led me to ask my previous physician for a sleep aid. He prescribed Ambien, which has two potential side effects: people who take it will often sleepwalk, and they'll use that trance time to stuff their faces. In my case, I'd get up and eat three peanut butter and jelly sandwiches between bedtime and breakfast. My blood sugar went nuts. So did my weight: I'm only 5'7", but before long, I ballooned to a hefty 212 pounds. Often, I had so much trouble breathing, I wondered if it was my weight or allergies to pollen and grass causing me to wheeze.

I should have anticipated this diagnosis, given my lifestyle—I've never been one to turn down a hamburger or fries—but it was still a shock. I was pissed when the doctor told me I had become a diabetic. What the hell? Now I had to watch what I ate and drank? What about those fruity tropical drinks I loved? I immediately began researching alcohol to find the drink that contains the least amount of sugar. (In case you're curious, straight rye whiskey is best, but tastes even better with a diet drink.)

Soon after my diabetes was diagnosed, I started touring the country to check on the 1,500 clinics we'd put into national pharmacy chains for Take Care Health Solutions. The part of my job I loved most was talking with the nurse practitioners we'd hired. In one clinic, which we'd put inside a Walgreens drugstore in St. Louis, a nurse practitioner asked me, "What would you have to accomplish here to consider your company a success, Hal?"

"Well, hopefully with better access to healthcare, life expectancy will increase," I answered. "I imagine that's what most people want, right?"

"No, Hal, you're wrong," she said.

Nothing new there, I thought. "Why?"

"Well, I volunteer in Africa every year, and I spend a lot of time with HIV patients," she said. "Their life expectancy is probably thirty years. What's most important to them is not how long they'll live, but how many *enjoyable* livable years they have left, which might be only ten."

That conversation provoked me to start thinking about how many enjoyable years I might have left. Being diagnosed with diabetes had made me acutely aware that my life clock was ticking down faster than I wanted, especially after my daughter Jessica said, "You know, I talk to you about your diet and your overall health because I want you to be around to walk me down the aisle on my wedding day, Dad."

Well, nothing like kids to make you crave immortality.

I often talk about the idea of enjoyable livable years on earth with my childhood friend Joe Sciolla. Joe had followed me out to North Dakota from Elkins Park, Pennsylvania, and built a horse ranch near mine. We agree that our goal as we near the end of this race called Life is to saddle up our horses, chase cattle across the northern plains, and ride together for as long as possible.

"My minimum goal is to be able to get on a horse at eighty years old without using a mounting block," says Joe.

"Mine is to distinguish one of my horses from one of my cows," I tell him.

Even on the anti-anxiety medication, though, this thought continually ricocheted in my head: *I'm going to die!* The thought of death filled me with dread. How could I live longer and better?

I'd been put on a medication to help moderate my blood sugar after the diabetes diagnosis, but it had to be administered via a daily injection. Lately I'd begun seeing TV commercials for a drug you only had to inject once every week. The ads claimed the drug was the most effective one on the market and featured people (presumably with diabetes) strolling through the woods and listening to birdsong. As an added perk, the ads promised the possibility of weight loss and lowering the risk of heart disease, which meant I could be more active in life. Maybe this was the solution.

These ads were beautifully produced. Most featured parents playing with kids and dogs or walking hand-in-hand around a pond at sunset. I was sold on this drug from its first airing and conditioned to want it more and more each time I viewed these beautiful, happy people clearly making the most of their livable years.

After a consistent month-long diet of viewing this ad every night, the drug—and, more important, the place it promised to bring me in life—sounded like Nirvana. With this new weekly drug, I wouldn't have to feel guilty for being a diabetic! At the very least, I could stop feeling like I was a chronically ill patient. Maybe I'd even forget about my allergy to tree pollen.

Unfortunately, my primary care doctor was still on vacation, so he couldn't write me this new prescription for the magical diabetes drug. He was also in the dark about how fast I was tapering off my anti-anxiety medication; three weeks had passed since I'd cut that dosage in half. But I knew how to get around that: I went directly to an endocrinologist and begged him to replace my daily diabetes drug with this weekly one.

The endocrinologist was extremely accommodating (to my nagging, probably) and called in a prescription for the new drug to my pharmacy. Off I went to pick it up, already feeling happier and more handsome. As the latest commercial implied, soon I'd be thinner and playing golf or basketball with my kids.

A few days after switching diabetes drugs, however, I began suffering from chest pains, difficulty breathing, loss of appetite, weight loss, and stomach distress. I tried to remember everything from that TV commercial's speed-read list of side effects. When that failed, I checked the list on the little informational pamphlet that came with the drug. Yup. I had every side effect. I was going to die from the new medication.

My heart rate went into overdrive. Maybe I'd die of a stroke first!

Then I had a new thought, equally unnerving: What if these symptoms had something to do with not properly tapering off my anti-anxiety medication?

To find out, I went online. Sure enough, the side effects of withdrawing from my anxiety drug *also* matched the symptoms I was experiencing.

A side note: the fact that I was relying on Google instead of a physician's treatment plan is par for the course. Years before the emergence of search engines, I had noticed that one of the fastest-selling books was the *Merck Manual of Medical Information* and recognized that our healthcare system was stumbling to its knees; people like me were researching our own ills. Today, Google has replaced the *Merck Manual* and, in a lot of ways, has also replaced calling a physician, since there are fewer providers available—a phenomenon we'll discuss in Chapter 7, "The Boys Club and Cyberchondria."

• • •

As the days wore on, my symptoms worsened. I was doubled over, short of breath, and suffered from both a loss of appetite and intensifying chest pains. My coworkers were wondering why I was cutting my days short in the office. Meanwhile, my family's eye-rolling reached Olympic levels. They'd heard it all before.

One night, I was watching a football game on television when I began sweating profusely. I headed up to bed, thinking I must be coming down with something. The flu! Didn't severe flu cause sweating, chest pains, and shortness of breath? Or pneumonia? I was too debilitated to even look this up.

An hour later, my symptoms were so severe that Renee called an ambulance. I was rushed to the hospital's ER with chest pains, breathing problems, stomach cramps, and vertigo. After receiving an IV, three nitroglycerine tablets to stick under my tongue to relieve the chest pain, blood draws, oxygen, multiple EKGs, and a chest X-ray, I was admitted for overnight observation and tests. A cardiologist would see me in the morning.

When I woke the next day, I signed a few releases and escaped the hospital to see my own cardiologist at another health system, the same one where my new internist was affiliated. "I've got you scheduled for a catheterization tomorrow morning," he informed me. "Meanwhile, just go home and take it easy. Oh, and here are three new prescriptions. These medications should alleviate your symptoms."

The drugs did nothing for me, so I kept Googling, which led me to conclude my pain and digestive distress might be caused by gallstones, an ulcer, or even stomach cancer! I immediately made an appointment with my gastroenterologist. After all, as an active audience member of the 187 commercials for about 70 prescription medications that had collectively aired almost half a million times earlier in the year, I considered myself an expert.

Through the pain, I laughed at the irony that this would be my ultimate death. My friends Stan, Harry, and I often fantasize about the worst possible outcome during our weekly Boys Club meetings at my home just outside Philadelphia, where the opening salvo for every gathering is a roll call of our latest fears from current maladies we're experiencing and options for dealing with them. If you're a Chiefs or Eagles fan, you'll remember how head coach Andy Reid would begin his postgame press conferences with "injury reports" and list the various injuries incurred during the game, followed by "time's yours," his cue for reporters to start asking questions. With all three of us being sports addicts, we became programmed to start our Boys Club meetings the same way.

Now, for me, fantasy had become a reality. I was really at death's door this time.

• • •

The next morning, I woke early for the catheterization, worrying about the catheter rummaging through my arteries and what they might find. The worrying was worse than the procedure itself, as it turned out, and the results were negative, although I still had my three new prescriptions.

Unfortunately, I was left with the same disabling symptoms I had been experiencing for weeks.

The following morning, I was back at the hospital once more, this time being prepped for an endoscopy and the fun of having a probe shoved down my throat. These results, too, were negative.

"Of course, this procedure doesn't take into account every possibility," my endocrinologist said. "You'll need an abdominal ultrasound to check for whatever the endoscopy can't see."

I realized with horror that he meant *my pancreas* was the thing he still couldn't see. Pancreatic cancer is incurable, in most instances—something I knew all too well from my constant Google searches, which could collectively be categorized as "Worst Ways to Die."

Knowing Harry was deathly afraid of pancreatic cancer, I arranged for a dinner weeks later with him and the head of pancreatic medicine at our health system, who confirmed over dinner that there still was no cure. This, of course, threw Harry's head into a tailspin, and we drove home together in silence.

A day later, I was back at the hospital. This time I spent twenty minutes with a technician rubbing my stomach with a cold jelly cocktail and a metal ball. The results of the ultrasound came back the next day. It, too, showed nothing.

I was becoming increasingly convinced that my symptoms might be caused by withdrawing from my anti-anxiety medication, along with the introduction of a new diabetes drug prescription, so I made an appointment to see a psychopharmacologist. After putting me through a battery of tests, he suggested that I resume taking the anti-anxiety drug at my previous dosage and see if my symptoms went away.

Still in pain, and now swallowing scores of pills to cover just about every possible illness and condition, I began focusing again on the side effects listed on that TV commercial for my new weekly diabetes medication. These side effects seemed to mirror those of the anti-anxiety drug I had been weaning myself off before, so I sent a message to my endocrinologist pointing that out. He immediately took me off my new medication and prescribed a different weekly diabetes drug that had only recently come to market.

When I tallied up the whole ordeal, which had started just after Thanksgiving and sent me into the uncomfortable zone of the unknown weeks into the New Year, I came up with four new drugs, six visits to two different hospitals, four specialists, co-pays galore, and an invoice that was being prepared for my insurance company. My company would then be forced to pay an astronomical bill for my care. Oh, and then there were the new lifelong prescriptions.

It occurred to me that I was becoming the single largest driver of healthcare costs, at least at my company. Yet, despite all the tests and care, I still had no answers to explain my stomach pain, loss of breath, or other symptoms.

Two weeks later, I finally got to visit my new primary care physician, Dr. Matthew J. Killion, MD, the internist I swear by, whom you'll get to know in Chapter 10. He quickly determined that the culprit was indeed the introduction of the new diabetes medication that I was so enthralled with after watching the television commercial touting its benefits.

• • •

How much did this episode cost my health insurer? Probably in the realm of tens of thousands of dollars, which would no doubt spark an increase in premiums down the road for both me and others in my group.

And for how many days did I put my family through hell?

That depends on which family member you ask. My boys, Travis and Kyle, basically told me to "get over it" and suggested that I see a shrink to deal with my hypochondria. They believed my symptoms were all in my head. My wife stood by me, concerned, but wondering if there was more to it than the change in medication regimen.

Meanwhile, when I retraced my steps on this particular

health journey, I felt a new urgency to combat, if not completely cure, my own hypochondria before I drove everyone around me crazy. That meant I needed to delve more deeply into the topic. For starters, I wanted to know how many people suffer from illness anxiety, and whether anyone's done research to find out why some of us are afflicted by near-constant health worries, while others sail blithely through the world without sparking a thought for the next illness that might come along and kill them.

CHAPTER TWO

The Making of a Hypochondriac

Recently I took a cruise to the Greek island of Kos, home of Hippocrates, and visited a five-hundred-year-old oriental plane tree there. This particular tree is rumored to be descended from the original plane tree where Hippocrates once gathered his students to teach them about medicine.

As I sat there cooling off in the shade, I thought about the fact that the word "hypochondria" comes from "Hypochondrium," a term that Hippocrates used to refer to the area under the chondros (which means "cartilage"; in this case, the cartilage under the breastbone), or the diaphragm. In other words, hypochondria is an obsession with what lurks below.

In my case, it's an obsession with the fear of dying, and with the diseases lurking unseen in my body that might kill me.

Are hypochondriacs born or made? Is illness anxiety the product of your particular roll of the genetic dice, or the result of something in your childhood or environment?

These questions are worth asking, because people like

me cost the healthcare system extra trouble and money. We're constantly making appointments for symptoms that feel real but aren't. We doubt our clinicians, so we seek second and third and even fourth opinions, asking for (or demanding) unnecessary medical tests, and running up insurance claims that help cause everyone else's healthcare premiums to go up, too.

Someone who is suffering from hypochondria and can't control their emotional responses to worries about their health will likely make an appointment with a physician or, even worse, will rush off to the ER. And, in today's minute-by-minute billing system, a physician has to account for every second spent with you as a patient. That means that people like me are costing our healthcare system, health plans, and employers beaucoup bucks, not to mention the resulting premium increases, which affect everyone.

"Why don't doctors just say no to giving tests to people who don't need them?" you might be asking.

It's not that easy. Sure, providers can say no to someone requesting medical treatment, but in our lawsuit-drunk country, many physicians would rather err on the side of caution and test people rather than risk a medical malpractice suit. Besides, since they're often restricted by healthcare insurers to allow only a certain amount of time with each patient, these doctors don't usually have time to drill down on interviewing patients and finding out what's really going on with them in a holistic way. It's extremely costly to know "for sure" whether someone has a particular ailment, and that cost eventually trickles down through the whole medical-industrial complex back to the consumer.

The thing is, I know all this rationally, yet I'm one of the worst offenders, a frequent flyer in the healthcare system. But why?

• • •

I wasn't always a hypochondriac. In fact, most people probably see me as a competent and successful urban executive, a guy whose happy place is my cattle ranch in North Dakota. At the ranch, I ride a motorcycle, drive a tractor, and spend hours with other cowboys, horseback riding while tending to our cattle, often suffering falls and injuries as a result. None of that scares me.

In fact, my friend Dave Bauman, who taught me to ride a horse when I first bought my ranch thirty-four years ago, and who taught me to eat a spoonful of yellow mustard if I suffered from leg cramps, just shrugs when I tell him I'm a hypochondriac. He'd never believe me if I confessed that my fantasies include someday building an exam room in the basement of my house, complete with an exam table, ultrasound and EKG machines, advanced video systems, and on-call technician so I can have my body scanned any time I worry about cancer. I also dream about having my own room at the hospital, one they hold in reserve for me when I need it, but otherwise make it available to others. (Yes, I know this is foolish. I won't do these things because I'm now a cognizant hypochondriac, one who has learned over time, and with considerable effort, that my fears aren't always rational.)

I did once try to talk to Dave about being a hypochondriac. He shook his head and said, "I don't see you that way. You've got no fear in you. You're not afraid of anything. Maybe you just go to the doctors more in the city because that's what people do there, or because you're bored. On the ranch, you're too busy to think about your health."

Dave reminded me of a time early on when he was out in one of his cow pens during calving season, and saw me walk into the calving barn. I was coming in to see how the newborn twins we had recently pulled out and their mama were doing.

"Unknowingly, I had put another cow who was close to birthing in the pen as well," Dave said. "I believe she had one leg out and was about to give birth. Anyway, when she saw you, she rammed you up against the wall four times and out the barn door. Meanwhile, I was calling to you to come out and help me, and you did. You didn't tell me until afterward what had happened to you. You had numerous broken ribs, but you never said a word about it. Just kept working until I saw you turn white as a ghost and asked you why. The very next day, you helped me put up lights in my barn!"

Dave also likes to tell another story whenever I start telling him I'm a hypochondriac. That time, he saw me get bucked off a horse. "The horse flew up one way and you flew the other way. You picked yourself up and never said a word. That's when I said to myself, 'This guy's not scared of anything.'"

These stories are true. Still, I wonder where my illness anxiety began.

I think I can trace it back to my fear of death in early childhood. I had the greatest family in the world, loving and supportive. Yet, for some reason, in early childhood I developed a fear of dying. As early as eight years old I used to lie sleepless in my bed, worrying that it was inevitable that someday I might die, and then what?

Sometimes I wonder if that was because we attended a synagogue every week where, at the end of each service, the rabbi read a list of hundreds of people who had died during that same week over the past few generations. It was not exactly the most uplifting experience, and probably why I try to escape before the death list is read. (Worse yet, now my synagogue has taken to sending e-mails announcing the recent death of another congregant, causing me to quit the congregation.) When I was a child, it seemed to me like the whole world was dying, and it scared me. That fear of "nonexistence" would sometimes overwhelm me to the point of causing a panic attack.

This didn't stop me from having a happy childhood and taking physical risks, like learning to ride a motorcycle at sixteen and playing club football in college. As a teenager, I also went to Israel a number of times to work on various kibbutzim. While I lived on one particular kibbutz in northern Israel, we were constantly being shelled by Syria and Lebanon, or shot at by Al-Fatah while working in the banana fields at another kibbutz near the Jordanian border, yet I was never afraid.

In fact, having met many survivors of German concentration camps there, I was inspired to drop out of college for nine weeks at age twenty-one to aid Israel's side when the Yom Kippur War broke out in 1973. I waited six days, since the last war was over by then, but this time the Israelis were overrun on the Sinai Peninsula and stuck in a fierce battle on the Golan Heights above the kibbutz I had worked at years earlier. Israel was losing, and it seemed clear to me that I had to go there.

There was a nationwide blackout ongoing when I landed in Tel Aviv. I proceeded to hitch a ride to a place in the north under cover of darkness. There, I was put to work loading and unloading military trucks, and learned to dart between shelters like everyone else whenever bombs were raining down from Syria or Lebanon.

It's true that I suffered from post-traumatic stress disorder (PTSD) after that experience. When I flew out of Israel and landed in Athens, I'd collapse in a heap if a truck backfired, or if a waiter dropped a tray and it clattered to the ground. The shell shock gradually receded within a couple of months, so I was able to return to college and graduate. Although I wanted to become a criminologist, I joined my father in his travel company because I recognized that he was working too hard and was beginning to feel the side effects.

Years later, I was aboard a plane at the beginning of a business trip to Japan when suddenly there was a huge bang and a lot of smoke. Apparently, the US Airways jet had ingested a flock of geese during takeoff and blown an engine. Smoke filled the cabin, and we had to make an emergency landing. The woman sitting a row in front of me was hysterical, but I remained calm despite knowing I had to board the next flight and continue my trip. My ranching instincts took over and I knew the best thing to do after getting bucked off a horse was to climb back on and keep riding.

It wasn't until many years later that the anxiety got the better of me. This time it surfaced as an extreme fear of the unknown. I was traveling in Vietnam when I suffered a bizarre out-of-body experience after visiting a museum that presented exhibits of the Vietnam war from the point of view of that country, showing the horror of death, the bombings, and the effects on Vietnamese cities. When these out-of-body sensations took over, it was literally as if I'd left my body and was seeing it from above. These experiences left me feeling highly anxious and sometimes in meltdown mode, and apparently also caused memory loss that still afflicts me to this day.

If you asked me, I'd say I consider myself a rationalist and a firm believer in modern medicine. However, from that point forward, I began fearing any disease I couldn't see, or imagining that I must have an illness that hadn't been diagnosed yet. Whenever that fear overtook my senses, I was in its grip and had no choice but to urgently seek medical help immediately, because my anxiety was bigger and stronger than I was.

A lot of hypochondriacs understandably hide their fears from other people, some more successfully than others. I wish I could do this, too. It's not something to be proud of, and it certainly doesn't endear you to people. But I've chosen to use my illness anxiety as a tool, sharing my journey through our health system to illuminate what's really there and what's not—and as a springboard for sharing strategies that can improve healthcare for all.

What Marnie Has to Say about Hypochondria

It wasn't until I started researching hypochondria with Hal that I realized how tough a subject this is, mainly because it's so difficult to pinpoint who has it. Few people willingly come right out and say they suffer from illness anxiety, even if they recognize they have a problem.

Luckily, Hal is an easy study because of his transparency about his hypochondria—although maybe he didn't actually have much of a choice. How else could he explain to me or our work colleagues why he suddenly has to exit a meeting? Or why we might see him through the glass walls of his office lying on the floor beside his desk, rotating his leg over his body in an effort to find out if his back pain is related to his kidney or a pulled muscle?

What I've learned is that even "cognizant hypochondriacs" like Hal have trouble recognizing that they have a problem with illness anxiety because they truly believe something is wrong with them whenever they feel symptoms. For them, fact and fiction are the same.

But let's start with the basics, and at least define the problem and look at some of the potential causes. Anxiety disorder (AD) is "the commonest mental disorder," with a prevalence of 31 percent in the United States.[1]

Illness anxiety disorder (IAD)—the official term for hypochondria as listed in the current edition of the

Diagnostic and Statistical Manual of Mental Disorders (DSM-5-TR), and the one most often used by clinicians—is one of the most commonly diagnosed types of anxiety, along with generalized anxiety disorder, panic disorder, phobic disorder, post-traumatic stress disorder, and obsessive compulsive disorder. A 2023 article suggests that between 4 and 6 percent of our population suffers from illness anxiety. However, researchers acknowledge that the percentage of illness anxiety sufferers "can reach 15 percent," with men and women equally affected and the onset of symptoms "most common between the ages of 20 and 30 years."[2]

For most of us, illness anxiety disorder usually begins in early or middle adulthood and may get worse as we age, with two main clinical presentations of IAD: 1) the care-seeking type like Hal, who seek out medical care, complaining of health symptoms and concerns, and undergo frequent diagnostic procedures; and 2) the care-avoidant type of patient who is so anxious about their health that they often try to dodge any sort of medical care. [3]

Either way, people with illness anxiety worry about their health out of proportion with reality, are overly vigilant about their health and prone to feeling depressed about it, and frequently monitor themselves for signs of illness.

Researchers have a number of theories about the actual causes of hypochondria. Some suggest that they're simply people who "have a lower threshold and tolerance for physical disturbances."[4] In other words, according to Hal, when his stomach hurts, "I feel the pain more than you do."

Many theories abound to explain the roots of IAD onset. Some researchers posit that hypochondria is a learned trait that begins early on when a child is exposed to someone else's disease. Others theorize that IAD is merely a variant of some other mental disorder, pointing out that 80 percent of patients with illness anxiety have other anxiety disorders, too, or suffer from depression,[5] although Hal is anything but depressed.

What we *do* know for a fact—thanks to the latest high-tech brain imaging available—is that the brains of people who are anxious work differently from the brains of people who are not.[6] When human brains perceive a threat—whether physically real or imaginary—a part of the brain called the amygdala sends out an alarm, telling our body's systems to prepare a defense reaction to the threat. Your hypothalamus then sends out adrenaline and other hormonal signals that set off a stress response. Your heart beats faster and your breathing quickens. Your blood pressure rises as you become alert and vigilant.

That's when your prefrontal cortex—the rational part of your brain—is supposed to kick in to analyze the threat at hand. Is it a mountain lion or an algebra test? Accordingly, the prefrontal cortex should amplify or dampen your sense of danger.

However, MRI studies comparing patients who have been diagnosed as anxious with other, "normal" controls show that, when subjects are presented with threatening stimuli, anxious people experience a heightened activity in the amygdala. The parts of their brains that should be shifting attention away from the threat and controlling the person's emotional response don't kick in as they should. An anxious person's sense of fear is therefore higher than the circumstance warrants. In other words, the brains of anxious people are hypervigilant to threats and perceived threats, causing those with IAD to respond with worry to events that others might dismiss.[7]

Patients with illness anxiety spend a great deal of time living in dread. Like Hal, they imagine that a headache is a symptom of a brain tumor, or stomach pains signal pancreatic cancer. They search for proof online, doom-scrolling through a variety of illnesses and usually settling on the worst-case scenarios.

For instance, not long ago Hal told me about a call from his good friend Harry. "He's even more of a hypochondriac than I am," says Hal. "He was taking his blood pressure for the fourth day in a row because he was headed out on vacation the next day and didn't want to be far away from home if he experienced another bout with high blood pressure."

Days earlier, Hal had spoken with Harry's executive assistant who, like Harry, had taken Paxlovid after contracting COVID-19. She had just shared with him that her blood pressure had spiked to over 160 and now Harry was in a state of panic because he too had taken Paxlovid after testing positive for COVID. Without having a negative test result for over two weeks after his first positive one he immediately went to get his blood pressure monitor and received a reading of 150/60.

Fortunately, Harry already had an appointment with his internist. With his anxiety in full tilt, Harry probably clocked the same miles per hour as his blood pressure on the drive to the doctor's office. After discussing his various maladies, the doctor took Harry's blood pressure. It read a miraculous 118/70. Relieved—at least for the next twenty-four hours—that nothing was wrong with him, Harry said he felt the color returning to his face. (About twenty-four hours of relief is the high-end limit of Harry's comfort level before some other concern takes hold of him.)

"When Harry relayed this story, I started thinking about how the relationship between investing in the market and hypochondria is rooted in our fear of the unknown. Investors invest in the future," Hal says. "When the future is unknown, many stop investing. Then, as the market begins to show signs of certitude, their anxiety recedes, and they begin making investments again because they don't want to miss out on the upside."

People who, like Harry and Hal, suffer from illness

anxiety disorder are dealing with fear of the unknown most of the time. They see the risks in the unknown and begin worrying. That anxiety can manifest as symptoms. In Harry's case, his relief came from the doctor telling him that there was nothing wrong with him. His fear of the unknown was eliminated, at least until the next day.

Without the temporary reassurance of a doctor who has just examined them or sent them in for imaging, the fear of an illness, real or not, causes Hal and Harry to panic, or even, in Hal's case, to suffer infrequently from actual panic attacks. Similarly, panic taking place in the market is caused by an event, real or perceived, causing what Hal calls "market anxiety disorder."

So how much do people with illness anxiety actually cost the United States in financial terms? Again, that's tough to itemize, simply because the research is scant. For one thing, there's a big difference between 5 percent of the population suffering from the disorder, as some studies suggest, and 15 percent, as others theorize.

One of the leading researchers on hypochondriasis, Dr. Arthur Barsky of Harvard Medical School took a stab at calculating the cost years ago. He reported that patients with unexplained physical symptoms with no actual medical basis account for about 16 percent of all medical costs in the country, amounting to hundreds of billions of dollars annually, saying, "Patients with somatization had approximately twice the outpatient and inpatient medical care utilization and twice the annual medical care costs of nonsomatizing patients."[8]

Barsky's study is out of date, but the numbers are still shocking. He and his coauthors claimed that the total healthcare expenditures in the United States were about $1.6 trillion. Extrapolating from their data, they said "an estimated $256 billion a year (16.0% of this total) is then attributable to the incremental effect of somatization alone."[9]

I'm sure the costs would be much higher now, since our annual insurance premiums, co-pays, and deductibles are skyrocketing every year. Each time someone visits a physician or ER for an unnecessary reason, that's putting a burden on the system—one that will eventually fall back onto all of our shoulders. And already people are struggling to keep up with their medical bills.

In fact, the biggest cause of bankruptcy for individuals in this country comes down to unpaid medical bills. In 2023 alone, "households containing 1.7 million people will file for bankruptcy protection this year" according to NerdWallet Health, and "about 56 million adults . . . will still struggle with health-care-related bills."[10] Sadly, the Affordable Care Act wasn't the panacea we all hoped. Today, most people are finding that their healthcare insurance—no matter what kind they have—falls short of what they need to cover their medical expenses.

Here's the takeaway: many people in this country are
struggling to keep up with their health insurance premiums
and medical bills, and hypochondriacs drive up costs. We've
got to figure out a way to do better.

CHAPTER THREE

Is Big Pharma Advertising Good for You?

I'm browsing online when an ad pops up.

"I won't let ulcerative colitis stop me from being me," says the handsome, curly haired actor. Then off he goes on a series of wild adventures with his beautiful wife and daughter: kayaking pristine waters, hiking up a mountain, horseback riding. Apparently this magical, once-a-day pill, Zeposia, will let him do all of that.

I want to be young and strong and travel to beautiful places, I think. *I need more adventure in my life! That guy's even wearing a cowboy hat like mine!*

But wait. Do *I* have ulcerative colitis? My digestion *has* been a little off lately . . .

Pharmaceutical companies are "mackerels in the moonlight": they stink and shine at the same time. Sure, they research and develop drugs that can save lives, but these companies also fan the flames of illness anxiety. How? By making us believe there's a magic pill out there someplace that can cure whatever we think ails us, and then selling us that pill. Even if you're not yet a doom-scrolling hypochondriac like me who goes online, ingesting every word with great velocity to diagnose some suspected malady, Big Pharma advertising might just turn you into one.

Or, as Tom Nichols wrote in *The Atlantic*, "If you wonder why we are a self-absorbed, querulous, neurotic society, it might have something to do with a barrage of ads meant to turn us into hypochondriacs who are determined to make our doctors prescribe us the thing we just saw."[1]

It's likely that you start each day the same way I do—with coffee and a handful of pills. According to *Consumer Reports*, more than half of all Americans take an average of four prescription medications *daily*.[2] That's far more than at any other time in recent history, and certainly more than people take in other countries. Pharmaceutical companies bear a large part of the blame for this.

Not long ago, I wandered back to my library after relieving myself in the powder room and turned on the television. A commercial for Flomax brought my attention to the state of my urine flow, something I'd never really given any thought to before that day. The ad was aimed at men with a questionable "stream," and began by asking how your flow is. The commercial quickly flipped to a firefighter using a water hose with a spray that could knock you onto your back. Then, to hammer home the point, the visuals jumped to a Yosemite Park geyser gushing water thirty feet into the air.

A few hours later, I returned to the toilet and couldn't help comparing my stream with the geyser and the fire hose. How many people, I wondered, would feel their flow was inadequate after watching that TV ad? If they were people with illness anxiety, they'd probably call a urologist and make an appointment. How much would that cost the health system?

Fortunately, when I'm out on the prairie with Dave and Joe, we simply drop trou to relieve ourselves. "Yo, Hal, nice flow," Joe yelled once, so I figured I now had someone other than a doctor to provide me with relief, if you'll excuse the pun.

You may be reading this and smugly thinking you're not prey to these ads. Think again. Even if you're streaming your television programs to avoid seeing any ads at all, ignore pop-up ads in the news feeds on your phone, and aren't busy surfing diseases and their cures online like I do, consider the televised 2023 Oscars program. Millions of us watched that event because we wanted to see the gowns posing on the red carpet, hear our favorite movie song, or find out who won the Academy Award for Best Picture. (If there's a wild event like Will Smith slapping Chris Rock in 2022, so much the better.)

However, while we were betting on who would win that Best Actress award, we were also getting ads for prescription medications shoved down our throats. Pharmaceutical companies like Pfizer, the biggest sponsor of the 2023 Oscars, spent $14.2 million on advertising during that program alone. Big Pharma also pulled out the big bucks during the Oscars show in 2022, with pharmaceutical giants Pfizer, Novartis, and Lilly airing ads, as well as the smaller company, Incyte. These companies all forked over up to $2.2 million a pop for a single 30-second ad.[3]

I'm a great believer in the wonders of modern medicine to keep people healthy. I applaud Big Pharma's ability to develop life-saving drugs that can help prevent strokes or heart attacks, as well as treat cancer and other life-threatening conditions. However, my journey through the healthcare system as a hypochondriac has taught me that there really can be too much of a good thing.

A recent CivicScience poll reveals that Americans have upped their prescription meds in the last few years, with 70 percent of people today taking at least one prescribed drug and 24 percent taking four or more.[4] Yes, many of the medications we take can save our lives, or at least improve them. But the fact that we have reached a point at which we think every symptom—or even every *hint* of an oncoming condition—needs a drug to fix it comes at a great cost, both to our health and to our healthcare system.

• • •

Once upon a time, drug companies relied on sales representatives who went door-to-door to clinics and hospitals to educate physicians about their new medications. Congress granted the Food and Drug Administration (FDA) the authority to regulate prescription drug labeling and advertising in the 1960s, supposedly ensuring that ads weren't false or misleading, and offering information about drug risks, benefits, and side effects.[5]

The first direct to consumer (DTC) ad was a Merck print advertisement for the Pneumovax vaccine in 1981, but DTC advertising didn't really explode until 1992, when a TV commercial appeared during the Super Bowl for a NicoDerm nicotine patch. Not long after that, pharmaceutical companies began fighting to legalize their right to air TV commercials. Since 1997, drug companies have used broadcast media to peddle their wares.

In 2010, a new law under the Sunshine Act increased transparency of financial relationships between healthcare providers and pharmaceutical manufacturers. In addition, physicians started restricting pharmaceutical representatives from directly accessing their offices and hospital systems, and have progressively tightened the policies surrounding that access. While headlines on gift-bearing, sample-toting pharma reps are often negative, they can bring educational value to doctors that can benefit patients.

Today, the pharma sales force is a shadow of its former

giant self. In 2008, 80 percent of physicians were accessible to reps. Now, "53 percent of physicians in the U.S. place moderate-to-severe restrictions on visits from sales reps," according to a report by the global sales and marketing firm ZS.[6] This has pushed Big Pharma to funnel even more money and muscle into DTC advertising so they can reach consumers directly.

The U.S. and New Zealand are currently the only two nations that allow drug companies to advertise directly to consumers. Without restraints on advertising, we've seen the money that pharmaceutical companies spend on advertising jump to nearly $10 billion annually, and it's still rising.[7]

According to author C. Lee Ventola, "The average American television viewer watches as many as nine drug ads a day, totaling 16 hours per year, which far exceeds the amount of time the average individual spends with a primary care physician [annually]."[8] Naturally, those Big Pharma marketing tentacles have expanded from television into the online marketplace as our culture has transitioned into a nation of Googlers.

The most common DTC pharmaceutical ads—and the ones subject to the most governmental regulations—are product claim ads. These mention the medication, tell you what it's for, then offer an extensive list of efficacy and safety claims to satisfy Food and Drug Administration (FDA) requirements. Before 2005, DTC ads grew at about 20 percent a year, or twice as fast as spending on pharmaceutical direct to physician (DTP) advertising, but now the industry is ramping up spending for online ads. This should come as no surprise, since searching for health-related information has become the third-most-common activity for people going online.[9]

While writing this chapter, with my television in the background, I have been barraged by over ten pharmaceutical commercials. They are omnipresent and won't recede until election season, when political commercials rule the roost and knock drugs off the air. I don't know what's worse. Maybe Big Pharma is being shrewd and letting the politicos drive you to their pain drugs at far less cost.

Oy, wait! A commercial for sciatica pain management just aired, and now my lower back and legs have started talking to me.

• • •

So what's the upshot? Are we better off having all of this information about available drugs at our fingertips, or not?

Pharmaceutical executives claim that DTC ads provide patients with information about new medicines and treatments for diseases previously considered untreatable. Several studies have shown that patients who have seen these ads will talk to their physicians about the drugs, leading to an uptick in prescriptions. The problem with this is that these ads are supremely well crafted and play on our emotions. They're designed by creative professionals who are experts at connecting with consumers on a deep, personal level, tapping into our desires to be immortal, or at least healthy well into our later years.

The reality is that too many people in the U.S. are taking medications they don't need, partly because of these ads, especially those of us who are already prone to health worries. The commercials target everything from toe fungus and diabetes to overly thin (or thick) blood, allergies, skin rashes, leaky bladders, and depression.

In fact, a cross-sectional study of 150 prescription drugs with the highest U.S. sales in 2020 shows that Big Pharma actually spent more money on DTC advertising to push drugs that were rated as having "lower added clinical benefit" to boost sales. That study also signifies that the strategy was successful, concluding that "direct-to-consumer advertising may increase patient requests for advertised products and the likelihood of their prescription by clinicians."[10]

To put this in plain English, more people asked their doctors to prescribe drugs after they saw those medications advertised. More clinicians were then apt to prescribe those drugs for patients who requested them, but *the drugs being prescribed weren't necessarily the ones with the biggest clinical benefits.*

That's a problem. So what's the answer?

For my part, I'm hoping to talk to my doctor about the nine medications I'm taking and have him slowly wean me off at least some of them. It's encouraging to learn that other people have done exactly that. According to *Consumer Reports,* "half the people in our survey who take medication said they had talked with a doctor about stopping a drug, and more than 70 percent said it worked."[11]

On the opposite side of this spectrum of the very medicated, there are, of course, the undermedicated. For a variety of reasons, such as lack of access, affordability, or a lack of health education, many people may not be taking the drugs that could really help them. There are also individuals who suffer from pharmacophobia; even when they're diagnosed and hold a scrip (prescription) in hand, they may be so riddled with fear of the potential side effects that they opt not to take the medication and search for alternative approaches to care.

Marnie's Way of Managing Pain

I fall into the conservative approach to taking medications, so I'm happy to see certain medical organizations, like the American College of Physicians, advise doctors to try more holistic approaches to treatment. If we could somehow convince the healthcare super-users like Hal that they don't need as much care and medication as they fear they do, and show the under-users why they need more preventive care and medications to keep them well, healthcare costs would probably level off to a point at which those with barriers could get adequate care at an affordable price.

Recently, for instance, I suffered a small tear in my shoulder. I was in so much pain that I couldn't lift my arm, so I made an appointment with a well-known orthopedist. He immediately suggested giving me a cortisone shot and a prescription for pain management.

Now, if I'd been suffering from illness anxiety like Hal, I would have taken that shot and that prescription. I might have even requested more imaging to be sure I didn't have cancer of the shoulder or something. Instead, I said, "I don't want that."

"Why'd you come in here, then?" the doctor asked, puzzled.

"Because I wanted to know precisely what's wrong with my shoulder so you can give me a prescription for physical therapy," I said.

The thing is, I know pain management is where the opioid crisis got out of control. People in other countries aren't popping pills for every symptom or to boost their energy the way we do in the U.S. They use alternative treatments and holistic approaches like physical therapy, diet, meditation, and techniques for lowering stress. A new approach to healthcare in this country could start with improving people's awareness of their own health and what they can manage themselves.

My shoulder was better within six months of physical therapy. If I'd disguised the symptoms with pain medication, I never would have done that work.

CHAPTER FOUR

If You're Not Depressed, You Should Be

School shootings, mass shootings, local shootings. China, Russia, Iran, and North Korea stoking fears of nuclear war. Banks collapsing. Inflation blues. Social media. Media in general. Extreme weather. Pandemic PTSD. Nefarious uses of artificial intelligence (AI).

Has our nation ever lived through such a depressing or anxious time?

Maybe. Ecclesiastes 1:9, a verse from the Old Testament of the Bible, reads, "What has been will be again, what has been done will be done again; there is nothing new under the sun."

I take this wisdom to heart when I think about the cyclical nature of life. It's a reminder for me that, no matter how much we advance technologically or socially, many of the problems and challenges we face as humans are not new. Rather, these are the same types of challenges we've faced in the past, successfully or unsuccessfully, often long before whatever crisis is rearing its ugly head right now.

Think about the threat of invasion that U.S. citizens coped with during World War II after the attack on Pearl Harbor. Or the "duck and cover" exercises schoolchildren did in the 1950s, when we were certain that the Soviet Union would lob an atomic bomb at us.

After that, there was the civil rights movement, Vietnam, the oil crisis in the seventies, and, well, you get the point. There are always global crises, personal problems, and reasons to feel anxious. So why is our national anxiety spiking? What's so different?

One big problem is that we can't just put down the phone or turn off the computer and escape the news. Thanks to Lady Google, the advent of AI, and nationwide connectivity, the phones in our pockets can take us anywhere, any time. There's no escape from the headlines. You want doom and gloom? You want to panic about something? Just peek at your phone or laptop.

I have had times when I've been too anxious to function, like the day I had to lie on the floor of my office because my heart started racing and I couldn't breathe. (I don't know why I always choose to lie on the floor, since I have a couch in my office, but somehow the floor is where I need to be.)

I was convinced I was dying (again). Fortunately, the transparency and culture of trust I've espoused and promoted among my colleagues also incorporated elemental design features like offices with glass walls, which I believe help promote accountability and break down hierarchical barriers. This enables employees of all levels to interact and communicate more easily. In my case, this also helped save my life, at least while I thought I was dying.

Plus, as we pointed out in Chapter 3, every time you go online or watch television, you're also easy prey for the pharmaceutical companies spraying advertisements at us like buckshot. Most of those ads are selling sickness, so they're designed to target our anxiety and create fear. If you watch enough of them, you can't help but wonder whether you have a disease you don't know about, worry that you aren't taking the right or best or enough medications, or even start thinking you're anxious or depressed—especially if you already suffer from illness anxiety.

In fact, now that we live in an age in which mental health is (thankfully) sliding off the taboo list of dinner table conversations, many of today's DTC advertisements *specifically target* our mental health, especially anxiety or depression.

If you didn't think you were anxious or depressed before, these commercials could very well change your mind. Rexulti, Cymbalta, and other medications developed to fight depression and mental health disorders appear on television with such regularity that it seems like the whole world must be anxious or depressed. Shouldn't you be, too?

The worst commercials—and the ones most frequently

aired—target depression. These ads show formerly depressed people (actors!) planting gardens, walking their dogs, and smelling the roses with orgasmic looks on their faces even if it's allergy season. If you see those ads while at the same time despairing over the daily news cycle, nobody would blame you for saying, "Hey, maybe I could be happier / a better parent / a more sparkling conversationalist/a more productive employee if I just took a pill!"

For instance, in one Cymbalta ad, you see a series of depressed-looking people: a young woman sitting alone in the dark, a guy sitting alone in his room even though his child is watching from the doorway, and so on. These people all look exhausted and glum as the narrator intones, over lovely clarinet music, "Depression can turn you into a person you don't recognize. Unlike the person you used to be. Someone your kids don't understand."

After taking Cymbalta, though, everyone perks up. The same actors are now going to work with smiles and makeup on their faces, playing with kittens, and kicking that soccer ball with little Jimmy.

It was only in 2014 that pharmaceutical spending on drugs targeted at treating depression broke the top 10 brand prescription drugs advertised. That's when Sunovion Pharmaceuticals shelled out a whopping $179.1 million for TV and print ads to promote the drug Latuda (lurasidone HCL). The following year, the drug Abilify (aripiprazole) also ranked among the top 10 most-advertised drugs, with over $107 million spent to put it into the hands of more Americans.[1]

• • •

If you're wondering if these ads really do have a significant impact on how many prescriptions get written for drugs targeting depression and other mental health disorders, the answer is a resounding yes—though the numbers might be hard to tease out, given the impact the pandemic has had on our mental health. (We discuss the overall health effects of the COVID-19 pandemic in Chapter 8.) Since the launch of Prozac in 1987, antidepressant use in the United States has quadrupled nationwide, according to the CDC, and antidepressants are the second most commonly prescribed drug in the United States, just after cholesterol-lowering drugs. Women are more than twice as likely as men to use antidepressants.[2]

Then COVID hit, and by 2020, Express Scripts Holding Company, a PBM, reported that the number of prescriptions filled for insomnia, depression, and anxiety increased 21 percent between February 16 and March 15, 2020, with the largest jump being for anti-anxiety medications. More than three-quarters of those prescriptions were brand new.[3]

For hypochondriacs, seeing these ads on television

is bound to trigger anxiety about our anxiety. We start thinking, *Maybe if we took this drug or that one, we too could be romping in the fields of flowers and smiling 24/7!*

While it's true that many IAD sufferers benefit from certain anti-anxiety medications—I'm certainly one of them—healthcare providers worry that far too many Americans are now taking prescription drugs that either might not work at all, or might not be appropriately targeted to the particular mental health problems of the person taking them. If you ask your primary care provider for an anti-anxiety medication—something far more likely to happen after seeing one of these ads, if you're a hypochondriac like me—chances are pretty high that you'll walk away with a prescription slip and hope tucked into your pocket.

In this country, adults make 30 million mental health–related physician office visits each year. Psychiatrists provide care at 55 percent of the visits, while primary care physicians provide 32 percent. However, among adults age sixty-five and older, and in rural areas where there are fewer specialists, more people see primary care providers for mental health issues.[4]

The problem here is that research on the neurobiology of anxiety is still in its infancy. That makes it difficult even for experienced clinicians well-versed in mental health disorders to treat patients for anxiety with the medications available. According to a 2020 review of treatment options, "The first-line treatments, SSRIs [selective serotonin reuptake inhibitors] and SNRIs [serotonin and norepinephrine reuptake inhibitors], were originally approved for depressive disorders and then later for anxiety disorders," while studies of newer medications "have been hampered by flawed study designs."[5] We still don't really know what percent of patients with illness anxiety are treated with effective doses, or anything about the patients who are potentially misdiagnosed or treated with the wrong drugs, since anxiety disorders have a high comorbidity with depression.

By the time a hypochondriac does get a prescription filled and gives that medication the ample time required for it to have an effect, weeks may have passed before they realize it's the wrong drug for them. What happens next? They call their non-psychiatrist physician, who spins the wheel again and selects the next drug for the patient to "try." Meanwhile, those of us with illness anxiety are not only hogging provider appointments but pushing up the cost of prescription medication for everybody while toying with our own health. We've got to do better.

• • •

Just how does increased prescription drug use raise our healthcare spending nationwide?

The most important cost drivers of prescription drug spending are increased utilization, increased average cost of medications, and changes in drug mix. There are additional factors as well, such as delaying the introduction of generic versions of drugs, and the higher cost inflation in the U.S. for pharmaceuticals relative to other nations.

In Chapter 3, we examined the overuse of prescription drugs in light of pharmaceutical companies pushing their wares through DTC ads on various television and social media channels, which causes patients who see them to ask their physicians to prescribe them—especially if they're like me and suffer from illness anxiety.

Drug costs are increasing, too, with brand drugs typically experiencing higher price increases as their exclusivity period ends and new brand drugs are introduced at prices higher than the drugs they're aiming to replace.

We pay a lot more for our drugs in the U.S. than people do in other countries, with per capita spending on prescribed medicine growing a whopping 69 percent just between 2004 and 2019, the most recent data available at this writing. In 2019, "the U.S. spent $1,126 per capita on prescribed medicines, while comparable countries spent $552 on average. This includes spending from insurers and out-of-pocket costs from patients for prescription drugs filled at the pharmacy."[6] The steep cost of medications contributes to high U.S. healthcare spending, and is passed on to Americans in the form of higher premiums and taxpayer-funded public programs.

This is partly due to our lack of a central negotiating authority. In the past, our federal government hasn't been allowed to negotiate prices for any populations other than Medicaid beneficiaries and military veterans. Bringing a drug to market can be an expensive process, to be sure, but the reality is that we don't have any good source that tracks the actual cost, so we (or our insurance providers) have to just keep paying top dollar for the drugs we take.

But perhaps that is finally changing. For the first time in history, under the Inflation Reduction Act passed by Congress, Medicare has the ability to negotiate drug costs to ensure lower costs and affordability to Medicare populations. Under the parameters of the new Medicare Drug Price Negotiation Program, the first round of negotiations was scheduled to occur during 2023 and 2024. These negotiations should result in prices that will be effective beginning in 2026.

As I've noted earlier, I'm a big believer in the magic of modern medicine to help us all lead healthier, happier lives, but increased prescription drug costs means a heavier burden on our budgets—as well as on the budgets of our insurance and healthcare providers. Whenever plan costs for prescription drugs start rising, our costs go up through higher cost-sharing and premiums. Tragically, drug prices are usually higher for uninsured people than for those with health insurance, because some payers can negotiate lower prices through their contracting efforts.

As someone with quite a long medication list, I have seen the prices increase firsthand. The most profound instance of this was with my diabetes medicine. I take a couple of different drugs to manage my diabetes after having tried many different ones over the past few years, all of which assist me in keeping my blood sugar down. As someone with a bit of a sweet tooth (how do you think I got to this place?), I don't always keep my nutrition in check. When I am really out of control, I find myself heading out to Hymie's Deli for schnecken or to a Wegman's for their apple pie.

If my wife catches me, this behavior can land me into a spot of trouble, so I usually preempt any cake criticism by coming up with a perfectly good explanation for why these goodies are in the house in the first place: Boys Club. The irony is that Boys Club sometimes meets a couple of times a week, and even though I am sucking down sugar, my A1C isn't going up, and *eureka*, neither is my weight.

While I watch my friends put on the pounds, I'm fit as a fiddle and get to eat whatever I want, thanks to my medication. So, it came as no surprise when I started to hear that the very drug I was taking for my diabetes was all over Hollywood as the new miracle weight loss drug. Rats, my secret was out. What's even worse is that the new demand for this drug is far outpacing supply. The result was twofold: not only did I now have to struggle to fill my prescription on time, but the cost of it skyrocketed.

What does this mean in dollars? My current drug, Mounjaro, isn't covered by insurance, and costs $1,600 a month since it's new to the market. Victoza, my first injectable medication, is $794 a month without coverage. Between 2015 and 2020, it increased by 42 percent and rose from $7,936 to $11,300 a year.

Ozempic, my undoing, cost me $631 monthly in 2018, jumped to $763 per month in 2020, and is now a whopping $935 monthly. It was approved as a weight loss drug in 2021, and when used for that purpose, costs $1,600 monthly.

So how can identifying and working with people who have illness anxiety help combat the high cost of prescription drugs?

For starters, healthcare providers should talk with us about "deprescribing"—cutting down or even eliminating certain drugs where possible. In addition, the U.S. government could also take steps to streamline the drug approval process. This would lower costs by reducing research costs and administrative fees. Encouraging generic utilization and making laws that would prevent brand manufacturers from holding on to their exclusive patents would also help the government tamp down soaring costs.

Finally, we should explore the possibility of making it simpler to import prescription drugs from other countries and negotiate or regulate drug prices more stringently.

Given the increased numbers of people in our country being diagnosed with anxiety disorders and depression, the human resources departments of large employers are homing in on strategies for helping their employees become healthier and therefore more productive. At New Ocean Health Solutions, for example, we've developed two new digital health programs, one for depression and the other for anxiety. Both of these programs are aimed at helping employees better self-manage their symptoms of depression and anxiety with digital tools and programs that replicate that kind of work done with a therapist.

In Chapter 14, we'll explore alternatives to anti-depressants, anti-anxiety meds, and other psychiatric meds commonly used to treat people with illness anxiety. We'll discuss cognitive behavioral therapy (CBT), lifestyle changes, and the use of relaxation techniques like meditation, yoga, and guided imagery to help people with health anxiety. Some have also discovered acupuncture as a means to lower health anxiety symptoms.

These non-drug therapies pose none of the risks or side effects of taking drugs. They have the added benefit of reducing prescription drug costs not only to those taking the medications, but to the general public. The bottom line is that we need to increase awareness among healthcare providers, insurers, and the general public about illness anxiety and the many treatments for better mental health.

CHAPTER FIVE

If It's Not an Illness, It's a Side Effect!

As I mentioned in the last chapter, I used to take Ozempic for my diabetes. This is the drug that really took home the Oscar in 2023 when late night talk show host Jimmy Kimmel joked, "When I look around at this room I can't help but wonder, 'Is Ozempic right for me?'"

His joke referred to the fact that so many people—not just Hollywood celebs—are using Ozempic *not* because they have diabetes, but because it can help you lose weight. Being thin is apparently still as much in vogue as ever. The famous faces that have admitted to using Ozempic or a competing brand to trim their tummies include Tesla CEO Elon Musk and former professional basketball player Charles Barkley.

Ozempic is one brand name of semaglutide. Semaglutide was approved in June 2021 by the Food and Drug Administration (FDA) to be prescribed first under the brand name Wegovy as a treatment for chronic obesity.

Back when I first started on Ozempic, the manufacturer, Novo Nordisk, repurposed a catchy pop song from the

1970s, "Magic," changing the words "it's magic" to "Ozempic." I loved the song, but used to sweat whenever the ad appeared on television because I knew the list of side effects was coming. Then I'd have to worry about whether my heart condition was causing my shortness of breath and rapid heart rate, or my diabetes, or that "Oh Oh Oh Ozempic."

But the TV commercial that wins the award for confusing the heck out of me with its list of side effects goes to Vascepa, a drug recommended by my cardiologist to help tame my high triglycerides. I had no problem taking it until I began having cramps and pains in my abdomen and wondered if this new drug, with its accompanying side effects, could be the culprit. Not long after scurrying down that dark rabbit hole of anxiety, a TV commercial for Vascepa happened to come on, followed by this warning: "Don't take Vascepa if you are allergic to icosapent ethyl."

Naturally, I looked up icosapent ethyl, only to discover its definition was simply Vascepa! I went back to my primary care physician, who told me to immediately stop taking the drug.

You really can't make this stuff up.

• • •

Many of us become so obsessed by the possibility of being

forever vital that we manage to ignore the insanely long list of side effects that's rattled off with each drug ad.

Is there another industry that can pull off such a dichotomous marketing plan and be as wildly successful as Big Pharma? In all my years in the travel industry, I never once watched a commercial for a vacation that featured a lucky man walking along a pristine beach with a beautiful, bikini-clad woman that was followed by a rapid-fire list of potential pitfalls for a romantic getaway: plane crashes, sexually transmitted diseases, food poisoning! Yet I'm constantly bombarded by advertising that lists miracle drugs and their side effects.

By the 1970s, the FDA started requiring pharmaceutical companies to issue warnings of side effects and risks associated with the drugs they were selling. Since then, more than 400 medications include "boxed warnings" designed to call attention to serious risks. DTC ads also include warnings of risks and side effects, as we've discussed, but it's tough for the FDA to keep approving record numbers of drugs and issuing the appropriate warnings. That's because approval programs have been driven in part by the 21st Century Cures Act signed into law in 2016 to help accelerate medical product development. According to an article published in 2022, "Although well intentioned, medications that are given fast track status are more likely to receive a boxed warning after they are approved. Of the 222 drugs approved by the FDA between 2001 and 2010, nearly a third had safety concerns."[1]

And guess what? The fact that those of us with illness anxiety see all of these warnings—hey, we're often actively *looking* for them—means we either worry more about the side effects than the symptoms we were treating in the first place, or we won't take the medications at all because we're scared of what the drugs might do to our bodies.

Over the past few years, a new phenomenon has appeared: commercials are now promoting companies that offer online or telephonic interactions that connect you with a doctor. You share your need, they ask questions, they ship you a drug in obscure packaging, and off you go.

Some of these companies have succeeded. Others folded when the government outlawed this practice for dispensing certain drugs. This pharmacy bypass has simply made it more convenient and less expensive than getting a scrip from your doctor. Is this good or bad? On the one hand, I think it's a good thing, since it provides access for patients. On the other hand, a doctor would point out interactions with other drugs you take, and insights not mentioned during the commercials. Nonetheless, it results in more drugs being dispensed.

And, either way, we're worrying ourselves sick. In 2021, CertaPet surveyed more than 800 people across the United States to find out what percentage of the population considers themselves to be a hypochondriac. The conclusion was that "health anxiety among Americans is increasing, as 75.6 percent of Americans have more health anxiety now than they did five years ago.[2]

While obviously we have to take these numbers with a grain of salt—CertaPet is in the business of certifying support animals for anxious people—the study results still interested me. The report continues, "regarding frequency, 63.5% say they experience health anxiety sometimes, 23.3% say they experience health anxiety often, and 3.45% say they experience health anxiety constantly." Not surprisingly, 14.2 percent of respondents claimed that "exposure to information about illnesses in the media is the leading cause of health anxiety."[3]

Yup. We're worrying ourselves sick, and those things we see online or on TV aren't helping us feel better.

CHAPTER SIX

Pharmaceutical Price Wars and the PBMs Behind the Curtain

It's easy to feel like we're crafting one of Grimm's fairy tales when it comes to the rising costs of healthcare, because there's a never-ending list of villains to blame: Big Bad Pharma with their clever sales and marketing strategies; terrifying hospital bills; and the penny-pinching health plans that flat-out refuse to pay for necessary treatments and medicines.

Big research firms like Kaiser are quick to blame the soaring costs of care solely on the marketing tactics of Big Pharma or the hiked-up costs of hospital services, but multiple players at work behind the scenes are contributing to creating this complicated, messy nest of skyrocketing numbers.

Think about the world of retail pharmacy. What do you picture? Probably bright fluorescent lights, endless shelves of medicine, and long lines of people waiting for their prescriptions at a pharmacy counter, where the persistent swiping of credit cards lets you know that people's wallets are being drained with the speed of casino addicts placing bets.

I had an inside look at this game for a good many years after being named president of Walgreens Health and Wellness division and senior executive officer of Walgreens Co. This was certainly never my career goal. My brainchild involved establishing clinics in pharmacies to offer more equitable healthcare to people struggling to find quality primary care in their neighborhoods. This was the basis for the business model of my company, Take Care Health Systems, which we designed so a patient could combine a clinic visit and prescription pickups in one place, while also buying necessities like tissues, shampoo, greeting cards, and over-the-counter (OTC) drugs.

Walgreens saw the beauty of this business model and acquired our company, which is how I ended up as president of their Health and Wellness division. At Take Care Health Systems, we were completely invested in healing, but it soon became apparent that Walgreens revenue depended on selling as many scrips as possible. Our seven hundred clinics and on-campus health centers certainly contributed to that booming business, although that was not our goal. Let me also state from the beginning that pharmacies themselves do not push drug purchases; rather, they distribute them.

From 2007 to 2012, I was responsible for $48 billion of the $63 billion annual revenue that came through Walgreens pharmacies. Retail pharmacy business is one that requires a strategic approach, especially when it comes to negotiating prices for drugs. This happens primarily through negotiating with pharmacy benefit manager companies (PBMs), where pharmacies, health plans, health systems, and others work hard to negotiate the best prices possible.

• • •

PBMs are the mysterious gatekeepers of the pharma world—think of the Wizard of Oz behind the curtain— who can negotiate drug prices on behalf of health insurance companies, retail pharmacies, government agencies, and so on. Essentially, PBMs hold all the cards when it comes to negotiating which drugs pharmacies can dispense and how much they get reimbursed for each prescription. As such, it takes two to tango, and this makes them powerful entities. The relationship they have with retail pharmacies, health plans, and employer groups is like a romantic courtship, but with fewer chocolates and roses and more spreadsheets and temporary separations and divorces.

Put another way, it's a delicate dance, and retail pharmacies must learn the steps of this dance if they want to succeed in making money on scrips while holding down prices. And then there are the rebates, which have become so multi-layered with each resale that many pharmaceutical companies are now issuing two prices to suppliers: one with a rebate and one at a lower flat price.

Walgreens was never up to the task of feel-good relationships. One of my first projects there as president of Health and Wellness was to change the corporate culture at headquarters, with the hope it would spread throughout the company. I started by making people feel comfortable—as in the very clothes they wore to work. Skirts and nylons, suits and ties gave way to business casual. My thought was that feeling a greater sense of freedom was bound to lead to greater creativity, better service, and profitability. However, a change in dress code, while symbolic, fell far short of my goal of fostering a more open, embracing culture of collaboration, and creating a place where people didn't come to work only because they had to, but because they *wanted* to be there.

But this was more symbolic of a bigger change. My real desire was to replace corporate politics, break down barriers between departments, reduce frustration, and create a more caring company. Unfortunately, this company-wide endeavor never came to pass. The company was eventually sold and senior management changes became the norm, thus stifling any chance for cultural transformation.

Negotiating with PBMs is about a lot more than comfort and charm, however. PBMs provide data and hard return on investment (ROI) when negotiating with the government, health plans, and health systems, which in turn negotiate on behalf of themselves. PBMs know that employer clients who are carving out a prescription plan need predictive analytics to anticipate the trends. It's like reading tea leaves, but instead of predicting the future, they predict which drugs will be popular next quarter, and which prices will rise or fall. Their tactics and resources are deployed in negotiating with both pharma companies and pharmacies. As a capitalist, I have no problem with PBMs, but rather with the value they bring—or more often don't.

For example, I never would have dreamed that the drug my doctor had prescribed for my type 2 diabetes two years ago would now become Hollywood's secret diet drug.

"I'm in telemedicine," notes Dr. Judd Hollander, MD, senior vice president of healthcare delivery innovation at Jefferson Health in Philadelphia, Pennsylvania. "One of the companies I interact with recently reported a four-fold increase in telehealth visits with patients reporting diabetes. They all want a semaglutide prescription for weight loss. This Hollywood trend has the potential to bankrupt the system."

As we mentioned earlier, today Wegovy is marketed to consumers as a weight loss drug, diabetes or not. I'm not against that, as those who truly need to lose weight will have an easier time doing so with medication, and losing weight can help boost self-esteem and combat depression. However, you can only negotiate from a position of strength if you're armed with this knowledge. Only then can you get the best deal possible and ensure that your manufacturers and their suppliers will deliver the right drugs for the right price at the right time.

Creating the balance among all of these players—health plans, PBMs, and pharmaceutical companies—is an ongoing issue that has a significant impact on patients and has opened the door for new companies that focus on providing drugs at a much lower price. Mark Cuban Cost Plus Drugs recently hit the market with a new approach, introducing accessible, affordable prescription medications. Whether this disrupts the industry is yet to be determined.

Health plans are constantly forced to look for ways to reduce costs, but that often means limiting coverage for certain medications. Pharmaceutical companies are pushing ads for the latest and greatest drugs, which may not always be the best options for patients. And PBMs still rule the roost with pricing that is kept above every stakeholder's reach. That leaves many patients unable to afford new drugs, resulting in low adherence rates.

With all these power grabs, it's not surprising that patients are often the losers. When health plans limit coverage for certain medications, patients may be forced to pay out of pocket or forgo treatment altogether unless their employers pay. This can lead to negative health outcomes, including increased hospitalizations (again increasing costs), as well as a lower quality of life. This obviously isn't the goal of health plans, but rather where they sit in the hierarchy of drug costs.

For the hypochondriac who has insurance coverage, this is a field day. In Chapter 11, we'll discuss a number of possibilities for addressing hypochondria, some of which I've tried myself. For instance, anxiety screenings and early detection of somatoform (physical symptoms of no organic origin) can help guide a patient out of the ER and into the therapist's office. We could also consider a "less is more" approach by taking a complete blood panel and full head and body scan to detect cancer or organ issues. Quest Diagnostics currently offers a complete panel for $300 and includes a virtual session with a certified doctor to review results. Blood tests are common, but scans need to improve on access and cost.

Here, too, is an opportunity: an entity that knows how to scale scanning devices will find themselves in a position to help bring down the costs of care, with hypochondriacs being a great consumer target. When this happens, I suppose health systems will make them ubiquitous, and health plans will cover the cost of full-body retail screening.

Another potential solution is to encourage greater collaboration between health plans and pharmaceutical companies, although the major PBMs are all now owned by health plans, so this may be happening without much notice. By working together, these stakeholders can develop more targeted and cost-effective treatment options for patients. Introducing alternative therapies, negotiating lower prices, or exploring innovative payment models are all possibilities. (God forbid—hypochondriacs would really put providers out of business with value-based care models.)

Through increased transparency around drug pricing and coverage decisions, and by providing patients with clear information about the cost and the effectiveness of different medications, patients can make more informed decisions about their care. Big Pharma's ads, with their endless lists of possible contraindications and side effects, don't, in my humble opinion, help me make better decisions about which drugs I should take. These ads only make me want to try different medications, while the side effects listed in the ads have the unhappy effect of making me pay extra-special attention to each and every physical sensation. So far, only a limited number of the listed side effects have truly affected me. Fortunately, death, a frequently mentioned side effect, hasn't been one of them so far.

• • •

At Walgreens, I made the decision to sell off our PBM the fourth year after I joined the company. Our PBM was one of the few, if any, that was a losing investment. I sold it to a company that had the fortitude and business acumen to make it well worth the price they paid for it, but I still believe in the power of direct negotiation, which is what we did at Walgreens. Rather than be competitors to PBMs, we negotiated between them, thus obtaining the best prices for our customers.

CVS (Caremark) and Cigna (Express Scripts, which previously acquired MEDCO), on the other hand, have perfected their moves. They have remained the reigning champions on the PBM dance floor as consolidation continues to mushroom, and vertical integration should prove successful for most stakeholders.

But we believe there is still hope. While the current state of healthcare feels like a daunting challenge, there is always room for a happy ending. Years ago, I founded the Convenient Care Association in order to ensure that the newly formed retail clinic industry remained on the up and up. Today there are more grassroots organizations and government agencies than I can count, all focused on promoting health equity, accessibility, and affordability. Ultimately, we all agree that the pursuit of profit should never come at the expense of human life.

Telemedicine, generic drugs, healthcare reform, and other initiatives appear to be working—or maybe it's a timing issue related to the pandemic—as strategies are continually being developed to bring down costs and provide wider access to healthcare. At the same time, healthcare costs are rising at a lower rate.

According to the American Medical Association (AMA), "health spending in the U.S. increased by 2.7 percent in 2021 to $4.3 trillion, or $12,914 per capita." This growth rate is substantially lower than 2020 (10.3 percent) and may be due to "the decline in pandemic-related government expenditures offsetting increased utilization of medical goods and services that rebounded due to delayed care and pent-up demand from 2020. Overall, health spending was 18.3 percent of GDP in 2021, compared with 19.7 percent of GDP in 2020.[1]

I'm confident that we'll continue to create innovative solutions and initiatives to make healthcare more affordable and accessible. These new approaches will surely address the overuse of services by people like me, foolish optimists who continue to believe in miracles, like, hey, I can lower my A1C without changing my eating habits if I just take the right drug.

I've spent a lot of time thinking about solutions to address the hidden costs of hypochondria. In Chapter 15, we'll delve into the root causes of these costs and examine a multitude of potential solutions to reduce or eliminate them. Additionally, we will discuss the importance of preventive care and how it can help mitigate these hidden costs in the long run.

CHAPTER SEVEN

The Boys Club and Cyberchondria

It's time for our men's night. Or, as our wives call it, "The Boys Club."

A few times every week, my friends Stan and Harry come over and we close ourselves off in my library to talk about anything and everything. I've known Stan for twenty years. Harry has been one of my best friends since elementary school, where we first learned how to hide under our desks in the event of nuclear war.

Our evenings usually start with a full-body survey of what's bothering us now. We have a sort of "HIPAA Enclave," as Stan calls it: a safe space to talk about our ailments and fears. Recently, the evening started with Stan. This was a novelty, since he's either the only one of us with no illness anxiety whatsoever or is a hidden hypo who won't admit it. I tend to think the former.

"I had to pass a kidney stone yesterday," Stan said.

Harry and I exchanged a look almost, but not quite, of delight. Stan is younger than we are by several years; still, it's about damn time he had *something*.

We discuss kidney stones for a good long time. Then Harry said, "Well, that's nothing. I have something wrong with my prostate. It's probably cancer."

"Oy. How do you know?" Stan asked.

"Because I Googled the symptoms and I have every one of them." Harry sounded confident. Almost proud. "I'm up at least three times a night running to the bathroom."

"How long has this been going on?" I asked, while trying to remember how many times *I* got up to use the bathroom last night.

"Two nights, now," Harry said glumly.

"In a row?" Stan asked.

"No, but it's happened twice in two weeks." Now Harry sounded defensive.

The conversation went on, but I was momentarily distracted, thinking about how Harry and I both suffer from cyberchondria as well as hypochondria. What would happen if Harry and I never looked up any symptoms or illnesses online? Would we worry less? Or would we worry that we're not at least checking it out, and worry more?

Most likely we'd give in and go online, since having the strength to avoid online searches for our health concerns would make us superhuman. Studies suggest that close to 90 percent of Americans Google their health symptoms before seeing a medical practitioner.[1]

In other words, pretty much everyone you know is

doing it, with the most commonly searched-for symptoms being fatigue, rashes, abdominal pains, headaches, and coughs. In a study of two thousand people, the most self-diagnosed serious health conditions included appendicitis, heart attacks, and brain tumors, with about 60 percent of people claiming they were "usually" or "sometimes" right about their diagnoses. About 47 percent of Americans feel anxious when they self-diagnose.[2]

For people like Harry and me, our illness anxiety means that surfing for diagnoses can quickly turn obsessive—and can lead us to burn up more healthcare dollars.

• • •

The first mentions of the word "cyberchondria" were made by British and U.S. media in the mid-1990s. By 1999, the *Wall Street Journal* had picked up the term, publishing a story called "Cyberchondriacs Get What Goes Around on the Internet now." In 2008, the word was a 2008 Word of the Year finalist in Webster's *New World Dictionary*.[3]

Several studies suggest that people with illness anxiety have a greater predisposition to being cyberchondriacs than most. People with elevated anxiety about their health are, not surprisingly, more likely to do online health information searches, which in turn makes them more anxious. In fact, even people without an existing illness anxiety find that searching symptoms online often makes them worry even more.

While it's definitely useful for most people to be able to look up their own symptoms and go into a clinician's office armed with information and questions, there are two obvious problems with our online symptom checkers. The first is that there is so much misinformation online. One recent systemic review of 11,000 websites reputedly delivering health and medical information showed that at least a third of them were of "poor quality."[4] Healthcare providers often have to start by disabusing people of the information they've collected before actually examining them, and that's sometimes difficult to do.

The second problem is that people who suffer from illness anxiety are even more apt than others to use the web as a diagnostic tool and fan their own anxiety. That's because more web content focuses on rare but serious illness, like brain tumors, instead of on benign explanations for the same symptoms. Or, to use another example, one pair of researchers found that the most common result when searching "muscle twitch" was amyotrophic lateral sclerosis, even though that's a rare disease.[5]

The internet is here to stay. Now, with AI, people will be looking up symptoms online more than ever—especially those of us with illness anxiety. The potential problem is deciphering what's real and what's not, which might drive hypochondriacs to the edge of online bipolarity. Accordingly, if healthcare providers admit that patients are going to look up their symptoms online—especially those of us who are prone to overuse the system—then they can potentially lower everyone's healthcare costs by simply giving their patients links to reputable online symptom checkers where we can get reliable information, research our conditions, and maybe even connect directly with providers.

As innovators of digital healthcare solutions, we at New Ocean Health Solutions have made a huge investment in personalized medicine—over $100 million, to be exact. We focus on chronic conditions, which is the most expensive part of healthcare. Our platform delivers on the need for improved health literacy and tools that empower self-managed care outside the exam room.

The majority of health and wellness solutions currently out in the marketplace make up a sea of sameness, with one-size-fits-no-one programs. Eat this, not that. Walk five thousand steps every day. In contrast, New Ocean Health Solutions puts users at the center of personalized health journeys that take into account their conditions, lifestyles, behavior, and willingness to change. We use intelligent claims analysis to learn more about users, and we have already completed the first phase of an AI project aimed at understanding how our users behave with our platform in order to improve and sustain engagement.

Our ultimate hope is that AI will streamline diagnoses and treatment plans that will improve health outcomes. The intricacies of mental health diagnoses and hypochondria generally may take a lot longer, and for good reason: the phantom symptoms associated with hypochondria are presented only through the lens of the hypochondriac.

CHAPTER EIGHT

What COVID-19 Taught Us about Healthcare

In March 2020, when the newest coronavirus was very new and little was scientifically known, or at least believed, I was having a hard time filling my lungs with air and my nose was running constantly. Having two comorbidities, I panicked and called my doctor, who appropriately sent me for an X-ray that showed nothing unusual. The symptoms persisted. Two other friends had minor sore throats and were waiting for other symptoms to arrive. They were certain this would happen within hours.

Meanwhile, my friend Harry called to say he was experiencing chest pain. "It's COVID, I know it is," he said, sounding panicked. The heaviness in his chest went away a few days later, but not his concern. The pressure on his chest began building again within a few days.

All of us were suffering from nothing more than seasonal allergies, as it turned out. However, for hypochondriacs like Harry and me, the constant coverage of COVID-19 in the media during the height of the pandemic convinced us that we were days away from being admitted to a hospital and placed on ventilators. We were certain we would die alone, or at least in adjoining hospital beds.

As time passed, the government mandates kept changing. Masks weren't required and then they were. Depending on what state you lived in, masks were only required in certain settings, like doctors' offices or on public transportation, or even left to individual choice. People questioned the value and safety of the vaccines. Many people began doubting everything government officials said, or we ignored their advice because there were never any clear and consistent explanations. Everything on the news was seemingly dependent on what news source you listened to; Fox News, for instance, carried advice about the virus that ran contrary to anything on CNN.

I grew disillusioned enough with government officials that my fear of getting the virus abated. Then, on a trip to Morocco, I started sneezing and coughing like mad, and became incredibly fatigued. By then I was all vaxxed up against the virus, including boosters, so I decided I must have the flu or some other, more exotic illness, given my location. (I came to this conclusion even though I'd announced weeks earlier, to anyone who'd listen, that I would "probably get COVID on this trip," since I had managed to dodge the virus thus far.)

Not wanting to disappoint my family, and frankly not

wanting to hear about being a hypochondriac, I decided to join them for a three-hour hike up and down the Atlas Mountains without complaining about my dizziness and shortness of breath.

Days passed. Finally, I decided to take a COVID test. When it showed I was positive for the virus, I isolated from my family, but didn't take Paxlovid (which contains the antiviral drugs nirmatrelvir and ritonavir). Why not? Because I'd heard that the side effects of that drug can be damaging. You know me, I'd Googled the hell out of them and figured I knew better than most doctors; if you've read every chapter, you know by now that's nonsense.

Ultimately, I was sick for ten days. My entire family came down with the virus, too, probably thanks to my son Travis, who was a COVID denier and had been partying with friends after coming home from Vermont Law School. He likely gave it to some of us even before we left the U.S. It then became "COVID Down the Lane" until the entire family spent our time in Spain and Morocco experiencing various degrees of severity. I had it the worst, of course. And that wasn't just because I'm a hypochondriac, I promise.

Should I have taken Paxlovid? I'll let you decide.

• • •

The coronavirus pandemic has been the single most important health event of the past century, and understandably fanned the fears of people who suffer from illness anxiety. Our anxiety was exacerbated by the fact that we were forbidden from doing the things that normally made us feel better, like seeing friends, going to our offices, or taking vacations. Socialization came to an abrupt halt, and our isolation during that time period still haunts our country.

COVID-19 cases haven't completely abated. By the time this book is published, cases may have resurfaced again, followed by another pandemic.

Either way, the first COVID pandemic continues to have a long-lasting effect on our country. The CDC estimates that, as of January 2023, 15 percent of all adults reported having long COVID, with 6 percent still suffering symptoms.[1] People with chronic conditions must continue to be vigilant even against the seemingly milder version of the virus currently circulating in our population. Meanwhile, I suppose those of us with illness anxiety are actively worrying that we're merely at the start of a series of rolling pandemics as COVID continues to morph into new variations.

We're right to worry. Despite the fact that the U.S. spends nearly twice as much per capita on medical care as any other country and claims to have the world's most sophisticated hospitals, advanced biomedical technologies, and skilled health professionals, we did a miserable job of preventing the worst COVID-19 outcomes. The pandemic exposed the ugly underbelly of the U.S. health system in a way nothing else ever has.

While of course I applaud the speed at which our government joined forces with private companies to produce effective COVID vaccines, I cringe when I think about how our privatized healthcare system and the U.S. medical-industrial complex continues to fail in delivering equitable healthcare. As Ed Yong wrote for *The Atlantic* magazine, our healthcare system post-pandemic has "effectively developed a chronic illness. Its debilitating symptoms are persisting long after its initial acute sickness and affecting every part of its body. And because they are invisible to the outside, they are easy to dismiss."[2]

Given what hospitals endured when the pandemic outbreak was in full swing, healthcare workers are now scrambling to play catch-up with backlogs of work. Patients who couldn't see their physicians during the height of COVID are now sicker than before the pandemic. Healthcare workers—especially nurses—have quit their jobs due to burnout, and a survey by the American Nurses Foundation showed that nearly 90 percent of nurses believe their workplaces are currently short-staffed.[3] This is especially true in rural areas.

The result of the pandemic is that more people are suffering from illness anxiety than ever before. It turns out that, in this new age of cyberchondria, an international pandemic stirred up a lot of health anxiety among Americans. In one 2023 survey, for instance, 75.6 percent of Americans said they have more anxiety about their health now than they did five years ago. Over 23 percent of the respondents said they experience illness anxiety often, and over 3 percent said they experience it constantly.[4]

* * *

One positive byproduct of the pandemic for everyone, especially those with hypochondria, was the debut of telehealth. This marked a significant shift in the entire healthcare landscape. Telehealth wasn't a new technology, but against the backdrop of the pandemic, it became the innovative solution that met a new need by ensuring medical access while minimizing physical contact.

The rapid expansion of telehealth services during the beginning of COVID-19 was especially remarkable in the area of mental health, especially since a check-in with a mental health worker rarely requires a physical assessment. Sometimes there are labs to assess medication levels, but mostly these types of visits can happen over the phone or in a virtual call.

A recent study across seven million adults with employer-based insurance investigated mental health claims made between March 2020 and August 2022 and found that in-person visits during the acute phase of the COVID-19 public health emergency (before vaccines were available) decreased by 39.5 percent. Remarkably, telehealth visits increased well over 1,000 percent, representing a more than 20 percent increase in mental health care.[5]

Claims costs were similar. Most of the mental health visits were for anxiety and depression—45 percent and 33 percent of the total visits, respectively—of which anxiety disorders saw the most vertical climb in virtual visits at 73.7 percent.[6] The rise in mental health visits reflects the reduction in stigma as well as greater access to care provided by telehealth. Part of the decrease in stigma is no doubt due to a number of celebrities—Kirsten Dunst, Katy Perry, Dwayne Johnson, Jon Hamm, Lady Gaga, and Michael Phelps among them—speaking openly about their own mental health struggles.

Prior to the widening of telehealth, many mental health patients might have gone untreated. Now we're bound to see a ginormous increase in medical billing. Patient costs of care are bound to increase, too, with scores of scrips for medications to treat anxiety, obsessive-compulsive disorder (OCD), and depression. On the other hand, those same patients, who never before managed to see a therapist for their anxiety, would likely turn up at the emergency department with varying degrees of symptoms consistent with anxiety.

It's not surprising that the World Health Organization reported a 25 percent increase in worldwide depression and anxiety during the pandemic.[7] Social isolation, gaps in care, and fear of infection were major contributors.

The OCD Center of Los Angeles says, "It is estimated that 4–6% of the population has clinically significant hypochondria,"[8] but this was exacerbated by the pandemic. News clips of people lined up in beds on ventilators and reports on sleepless healthcare providers stretched too thin left many people with an intense fear that they would be diagnosed with another serious condition. After all, most of those who died had comorbidities, often untreated chronic conditions due to health illiteracy and inequity. The pandemic drove hyper-awareness about disease, but also shone a bright light on our inadequacies to treat, which has only raised our levels of illness anxiety.

While the U.S. has done an admirable job in developing increasingly sophisticated drugs and ushering in techno-logical breakthroughs in healthcare, our preoccupation with instant cures has kept us from putting any real energy into public health. The COVID-19 pandemic served to illuminate shortages in basic medical equipment, staff, and hospital beds, as well as to show the disproportionate effects of disease on the most vulnerable populations.

For instance, neither the risks of infection nor the statistics of suffering severe illness were equal across populations; rather, those outcomes depended on socioeconomic factors such as housing status, environmental vulnerability, type of employment, and chronic health conditions like diabetes, obesity, and respiratory illness. People of color and those living in poverty suffered more losses during the pandemic largely due to having less access to healthy food, clean water, high-quality housing, and easily accessible (and affordable) healthcare.

The bottom line is that we can't blame COVID-19 as the only reason for the crisis in healthcare, because the crisis was already in full bloom. A healthcare system that wobbles during the best of times is hardly going to stand strong during public health emergencies. Our privatized, market-based healthcare system was poorly equipped to respond effectively during the pandemic. If we don't do something to fix this fractured, crumbling system, the next pandemic (and there *will* be one) will hit us even harder.

While I might sound a bit pessimistic, I actually have faith in our ability as Americans to come together and find a way to vastly improve our healthcare system, but that will take a renewal of politicians finding common ground and working in sync with the private sector.

Okay. Maybe I should be pessimistic after all.

• • •

Will I behave differently during the next pandemic?

Probably not. I'm a cognizant hypochondriac, so if the government tells me again that I have to wear a mask to protect myself, I won't do it. If I feel others would feel more comfortable if I do wear a mask, though, I will. I'll probably get any vaccine being offered, but I might not try to crash the line to get the first one out of the box.

This isn't because I trust our government's healthcare agencies, or because it was shown to be politicized, but simply because I believe the vaccine can't hurt. Remember, I was quadruple-dosed and current with my COVID vaccines and still contracted the virus on that family trip to Morocco. At the same time, I know it was likely that I might have been far more ill if I hadn't had the vaccine.

I hope that our healthcare system will take our COVID lessons to heart. We desperately need to address the existing health disparities that low-income and ethnic minority communities experience. Our country has created an Emergency Medical Treatment and Active Labor Act to ensure that anyone can receive emergency healthcare, regardless of their ability to pay for it, but there is no such program to ensure preventive or primary care. Hospitals need to honor all patients by ensuring that their organizations promote equity and inclusion both in employment policies and in patient care.

The U.S. currently structures healthcare "as the product of millions of interactions between physicians and their patients," as William Sage writes in his article "What the Pandemic Taught Us: The Health Care System We Have Is Not the System We Hoped We Had" for the *Ohio State Law Journal*.[9]

He notes that "from mask resistance to vaccine hesitancy, the American experience with COVID-19 shows that tension between individual choice and the collective interest is an endemic problem in U.S. public policy, which the dyadic, physician-dominated approach to health policy accentuates." We would be far better off if we addressed the social problems "that bear on health without medicalizing them,"[10] as he puts it. I couldn't agree more.

Marnie's View of Hypochondria and the Future of Healthcare—from Hal's Front Porch

As Hal pointed out earlier, one good thing to come out of COVID-19 is the new acceptance of telemedicine by both the public and healthcare workers. Telemedicine was viewed with some skepticism before the pandemic, with many saying there was no way to provide quality care through digital media. That attitude has mostly been erased now that many more people have experienced telemedicine on both sides.

For our part, at New Ocean we've addressed some of the healthcare inequities highlighted during the pandemic by providing solutions to address underlying conditions. We currently combine our existing digital chronic disease management programs with lifestyle programs for holistic healthcare plans, providing a first-of-its-kind mobile health management tool designed for everyone fighting not only COVID-19, but subsequent viruses to come. Our solution opens access to everyone through mobile technology, reducing social inequities to care. It's the least we can do.

Bringing this to market in the midst of a very crowded space has been the hardest part but having 24/7 access to care from providers in the form of live, telehealth, AI coach–enabled, and digitally directed coaching is where we see the future.

Healthcare's highflyers are people with illness anxiety like Hal. He has multiple chronic conditions, and because of his hypochondriac response to every little change and fluctuation (ahem . . . it's called being human), he needs a constant connection to his healthcare providers. That's why he has signed up for concierge healthcare, as you'll see in Chapter 10, which is devoted to that subject.

Recently, I went out to the ranch to work with Hal. The executive team retreats here to hold business meetings. For me, a native East Coaster, this is truly a social distancing experiment. From Hal's ranch in North Dakota, it's five miles to the nearest paved road, and his closest neighbors are miles away. When I finally arrive after flying from Philadelphia to Minnesota, where I wait two hours for a connecting flight to North Dakota, followed by an hour-long ride to Linton, I have to say the ranch is probably the most productive and soothing environment I've ever experienced. I can see why Hal's hypochondria dissipates there.

Settling in at the ranch makes you feel like you're moving in slow motion. Yet it's really the opposite. Without all of the other external media, disruptions of traffic, crowds, and chatter, I'm actually able to move faster and think more clearly. One time I went to Linton and our team put together a new business plan over the course of just two days because Hal had brought us to a place where we could focus solely on the business initiatives.

It was during that meeting two years ago that we made the decision to invest in AI at New Ocean Health Solutions. Back home, it took us an additional two months to refine our business plan and another year to start phase one of AI. This phase focuses on keeping people engaged in our solution by identifying the preferences and behaviors of those who are registered to our user-facing mobile health management tool, which we named The Voyage.

In a lot of ways, The Voyage was inspired by Hal's own journey, because his health is under his continuous assessment—if not through his own checklist of symptoms and meds, his Apple Watch and Dexcom G6 continuous glucose monitor, which provide results that trigger self-motivated calls to actions that improve and maintain his health. Likewise, The Voyage combines a whole-health design with technology to empower individuals to better self-manage their health risks outside of the emergency room and provider's office. The Voyage approach is less anxiety-inducing than meeting with white coats in a sterile exam room, though, because it's built with digitally directed coaching that confidentially and confidently guides users to take small steps to get in control of their health.

For example, after recognizing that your blood sugar is high, The Voyage will trigger a message that contains evidenced-based treatment. If a week goes by with no improvement, The Voyage suggests that you make an appointment with your provider and gives you a link to the scheduler right there in the palm of your hand.

It's an instantly accessible coach, though available through software rather than human, and it's designed to identify health risks and engage a person on a journey toward healthier living. Phase two, which is intended to include an AI chatbot and to allow for two-way communication between users and coach, was expected to be launched in 2024.

Hal often states that his life's work has been all about creating solutions for unknown, unmet needs. This was one of them. By the time the pandemic revealed the magnitude of health inequities and barriers to care, our mobile health management platform was already built as a scalable solution to stratify risk and extend self-managed care into the community and home. We don't believe we will ever replace doctors, but we're working on tightening the gaps in care and becoming an alternative solution.

Even better, providing this digital health coach can go a long way toward reassuring people with illness anxiety about their symptoms, keeping them out of emergency rooms and providers' offices. This has the potential to cut down healthcare costs for all.

In my role as chief marketing and strategy officer for New Ocean, I work with Hal and other executives to advance the company's vision and execute strategic business initiatives. Day-to-day marketing involves creating content to drive brand awareness, advertising that targets key decision makers, and campaigns that generate qualified leads through paid promotion of this content. The content creation can be a whole lot of fun, especially when your boss is not risk-averse to bold ads with disruptive headlines.

For instance, we once produced a video explaining why our private health assessment is better than other health risk assessments (HRAs) on the market. For starters, it's shorter, and asks noninvasive questions that don't require having the right medical information on hand. It doesn't need to be filled out in one sitting, and it's designed with behavioral science to identify not only risk but also a patient's readiness for change, producing results that take you on a personalized holistic health journey through the programs in The Voyage.

The video we produced was titled "Shame," and it started with footage of someone sitting at a computer and taking a traditional health assessment. "How often do you cry?" say the words on the screen, which triggers a voice-over saying, "Do traditional health assessments and questions leave you feeling a little exposed?"

The camera then pulls out to a wider action shot of everyone in the office performing their jobs naked. (They were actually wearing nude underwear, but our editors fogged the footage by pixelating the "exposed areas.") Ads like these, along with other rich sales marketing campaigns and collateral, fill our own channels, and we also use them to deliver paid and earned media.

Last week was my fifth time out to the ranch since I started working with Hal. We were there to produce a new video marketing series, so we had brought in a camera crew and invited guests for a three-day production shoot for a video that aims to provide inspiration and insight into timely topics that are relevant to C-suite and human resources executives, as well as to benefits decision makers.

We had already shot five of these interviews in Hal's

library in his Pennsylvania home. This next set included a couple of healthcare executives: Dr. Judd Hollander, MD, senior vice president of healthcare delivery innovation at Jefferson Health in Philadelphia, Pennsylvania; and Lukas Fischer, BSN, chief executive officer of Linton Regional Medical Center in North Dakota.

Some of Hal's friends and colleagues were around, too: neighbor and cattle rancher Dave Bauman; real estate executive Joe Sciolla of Cresa Partners; private equity healthcare executive Greg Moerschel, managing director of Beecken Petty; and venture capitalist Dave Twersky. With the exception of Judd and the crew, Linton was "home" to everyone present. They were either born and raised here, transplanted, or have been living here part-time for decades. Hal and I had gathered these people together so they could share insights into how they lead their businesses and the thoughts behind them. They weren't the typical thought leadership questions, because Hal doesn't think that way.

They were all brilliant during the interviews, but some of the most memorable soundbites came from the sharp contrast of responses between city doctor Judd Hollander and Lukas Fischer, who works in rural Linton.

"What are the greatest challenges you find in healthcare?" I asked them at one point.

"We just don't have enough doctors," Lukas said.

"Right," said Judd. "Our shortages are nothing compared

to what is happening here. In the city, where we don't have a physician shortage, we still have an appointment shortage, but there's also the convenience of the emergency room, where you can get all your tests done instead of waiting for an appointment." (In Chapter 9, we'll share why Judd calls the emergency room "the big box retailer of healthcare.")

The interviews also gave me a new appreciation for Hal, as I saw him listen attentively to the responses he received from his light peppering of questions. He is a complex individual. Hal is clear minded in the three-dimensional chess moves he plays in business. However, all his logic evaporates when it comes to his hypochondria. During the times he suffers from bouts of acute illness anxiety, things can fall apart fast, as I witnessed during this work session.

Over the course of three days on the ranch we completed six interviews, one cluster panel, numerous wardrobe and set design changes, intakes and outtakes. We also shot B-roll footage of the sunrises and sunsets, Red Angus cattle, horses, and hay bales. Meanwhile, Hal continued completing all the regular chores that come with running a ranch, starting at sun-up with feeding his horses.

By Friday evening, Hal looked exhausted. A storm was setting in, yet he had invited twenty-two people—friends, family members, and neighbors—to our wrap party, a barbecue with twenty-two rib-eye steaks. Each family brought their favorite sharable food as well, which meant tubs, trays, and bowls of homemade salads, pizza, secret recipe cookies, and brownie bars. The house filled with happy chatter while Hal's neighbor, Wayde Bauman, stood under the covered porch grilling steaks to perfection and the rest of us were somewhere around the ranch house, celebrating the successful end of the shoot.

Eventually, Hal came in to take his seat at the table. He remained silent, however, and disappeared halfway through eating his steak. Fifteen minutes later I felt my wrist buzzing. It was my Apple Watch ringing, since my phone was in my computer bag at the other end of the house.

When I looked down the table, I realized Hal was gone. Where was he? I tapped my watch and saw he was calling me. I got up quickly from the table and went to a corner of the room, where I stood talking into my watch and feeling both alarmed and ridiculous.

"Hal, what's wrong?"

I had to hold my watch to my ear to hear him over the buzz of conversation around the dinner table. "Look, Marnie, don't make a big deal, but please get Judd and come to my room."

Uh-oh. Were we doing the "Hypo Man" routine?

No, I decided. We were here at the ranch, Hal's happy place. Besides, I'd noticed how tired Hal had looked at five o'clock with guests coming at six. Maybe this was an actual emergency.

I found Judd deep in conversation about the failure of value-based care systems at one end of the table. "The definition of value-based care means not paying," he was saying.

"Judd," I said. "Sorry to interrupt. Can you please come with me?"

"What?" He looked confused.

"It's Hal," I said, and then regretted it. That was less than discreet.

Immediately everyone at the table wanted to know if Hal was okay.

"Fine, I think," I said, thinking of how isolated we were out here on the ranch. I felt like a flight attendant in mid-air calling for any doctors on board to handle a medical emergency.

Judd and I hurried down to the master suite and found Hal sprawled on top of his bed in his dungaree overalls with a blood pressure monitor hooked up to his arm.

"There's something wrong," he gasped. "You have to help me."

Judd immediately went into ER mode. "What are you feeling, Hal? Tell me what's going on."

Uh-oh. This was serious. I looked down at Judd's feet as he was shifting closer to Hal and took note of his new cowboy boots as Judd took one of Hal's wrists.

We were all silent. For a split second, though, I couldn't

decide if I was on candid camera, or whether Judd looked like a doctor playing a cowboy or a cowboy playing a doctor.

I finally decided that Judd really was playing Billy Crystal in *City Slickers*. But Hal definitely wasn't Jack Palance doing his one-armed push-ups on stage after winning the Academy Award. Hal was acting like a centurion on his death bed.

"Your pulse is fine, Hal," Judd said after a few minutes.

"It is?" Hal asked in disbelief. "No, it can't be! My blood pressure is 187 over 92. My watch said it was 212!"

"Did you eat?" Judd asked, sounding a little more concerned.

"Yes, a little. But I don't have an appetite."

"See? It's the diabetes drugs!" I said in my "eureka!" voice. "The drugs you're taking are appetite suppressants that throw you into hypoglycemia. The same thing can happen with crash diets. Hal, tell Judd how many diabetes management drugs you're taking," I said.

"Four," Hall said sheepishly.

"So maybe you should discuss these drugs with your doctor."

"Judd *is* a doctor," Hal countered.

"Have you been staying hydrated?" Judd asked.

"Yes, that's all I have been doing all day," Hal said. "Do you want to take my blood pressure again?"

"I will if you want me to," Judd said. "But we tell people

that the worst thing to do is to repetitively keep taking your blood pressure. It makes you anxious."

"Do it anyway," Hal said. "Please."

Judd wrapped the cuff around Hal's arm. Hal was breathing heavily now. "Do you feel short of breath?" Judd asked.

"No," Hal said.

"Well, why are you breathing that way?" Judd asked.

"He's anxious," I said.

"No, I'm not anxious," Hal said. "I take anxiety meds for that." He started to laugh, and we did, too.

Wait a minute, I thought, and said, "Hal, is this a joke?"

"No! My blood pressure is high." He looked insulted.

The machine hummed. After 30 seconds, Judd said, "Hal, it's 167 over 82."

"Well, isn't that too high?" Hal asked.

"No. Your blood pressure fluctuates. That's nothing to worry about right now."

"I'm fine?" Hal looked slightly reassured. "So, I don't have to lay here?"

"No," Judd said.

Hal rocked his feet down to the floor and stood up tall. Right then and there, I knew I had just witnessed in real time the entire *raison d'etre* for this book.

"Hal, is this the culmination of a long couple of days of

nerve-wracking interviews?" I asked gently. "Are you feeling anxious? Or is it because you've been flying on automatic pilot and out here, you're finally able to exhale and . . ."

Hal cut me off. "No. I'm not anxious except about my blood pressure being that high."

I finished my thought anyway. "Okay, then maybe you really are taking too many medications because of what you've seen advertised on television."

He didn't answer.

In my view, Hal's hypochondria, or illness anxiety, sometimes doesn't seem any more real to me than his diabetes. He looks fit as a fiddle whenever he's bounding through the office with his latest unremarkable lab results, a sort of hypochondriac report card that earns him a cookie or an approval stamped "healthy." But on the inside, he's a diabetic kept in control by meds. What's more, he will do anything to avoid becoming sick and dying, and that obsession is precisely what fans the flames of his condition and hundreds of events like this.

After the episode on the ranch, Judd and I looked at each other and smiled after Hal, who clearly felt relieved, left the room and headed for a piece of cherry pie.

"Is this the real reason why I was invited to participate in the CEO series?" Judd asked. "Because Hal's concierge doc couldn't make it?"

I couldn't answer that.

CHAPTER NINE

Why the ER Is the Big Box Retail Store of Healthcare

Just as most people never forget their first kiss, I'll never forget my first trip to an emergency room. I was twelve years old and excitedly looking forward to having what I was certain would be the summer of my life, touring and hiking national parks with other boys my age.

As it turned out, it was a miserable experience. After departing Philadelphia and being jammed for days in a station wagon with seven other kids and two adults, we arrived in the Grand Tetons, where I was overwhelmed by abdominal pain and flown to a Denver hospital for a potential appendectomy.

My parents quickly secured tickets and flew from Philadelphia to Denver to be there for the operation. I was brought into the hospital emergency room hours ahead of them, unaware of the cause of my omnipresent pain.

By the time my parents were reunited with me in the ER, my terror had morphed into red-faced humiliation.

"Hey," I said with a sheepish look on my face when they found me.

My parents turned to the doctor, who said, "Hello, Mr. and Mrs. Rosenbluth. Your son will be fine. He was just suffering from not moving his bowels for days, but it's all good now. You're free to take him home if you wish."

Fast-forward to my freshman year at the University of Miami, when I was rushed off the football field with similar symptoms and taken to the emergency room at Doctors Hospital in Coral Gables, Florida. There, they found that my appendix had ruptured on the field and immediately operated, apparently saving my life. (Needless to say, my folks didn't dare head to the airport for a repeat performance.)

These layered experiences of pain, fear, reassurance, and relief lay the groundwork for the emergency room (ER) of a hospital to become my go-to happy place as an adult. Whenever I experienced an inexplicable physical discomfort—headaches, stomach pains, mysterious back-aches, dizziness, a racing heart—I could count on the ER being open 24/7 to save me from dying—or at least from worrying.

The feeling of being discharged with a nothingburger was always the best of all possible outcomes for me, even if, like most hypochondriacs, that sweet sense of relief lasted only until the next bout of anxiety. Of course, every time I use the services of a hospital ER for what turns out to be no reason, as I shared in the first chapter when I went rushing off to get checked out for anthrax poisoning, I'm costing myself—and every other healthcare consumer—unnecessary money. A *lot* of unnecessary money. And that's a problem.

According to the most recent CDC statistics available, over 139.8 million Americans visit hospital emergency rooms each year.[1] This translates to 42.7 visits for every 100 people. Of the people who are seen by an ER, only about 13 percent end up being admitted to hospitals. Not surprisingly, the ER visit rate for patients with private insurance was the lowest, while people who are on Medicaid or other state-based programs had the highest emergency room visit rate compared to other expected payment sources.

What do these numbers tell us? It's tough to tease out how many people with health anxiety are driving up the number of ER visits, because there isn't enough research available that reflects that number. But these statistics still reveal that a lot of people in the U.S. are going to the ER when they could be seen by a primary care doctor or an urgent care center provider instead—and that's a real wallop to our healthcare system, both cost-wise and to the quality of care we can deliver.

One problem is that emergency rooms aren't really set up to be "first come, first served," so patients end up waiting longer. You might have a fever, but despite having already signed in with the triage nurse and waiting fifteen minutes, if a car accident victim comes in, you'll be pushed down the line, and rightfully so. Wait times at urgent care clinics typically range from minutes to an hour, while patients in a busy ER can be sitting there two, three, or more than four hours, depending on who else shows up and what they're presenting with.

There's a domino effect that starts even sooner than that. Misuse or overuse of 911 calls for nonemergencies carries the risk of overwhelming emergency medical system services and threatens to increase ambulance wait time. This adds costs to municipal services. In addition, delayed EMS response time increases the risk to patients waiting for help.

As people stack up in the ER, wait times lengthen, contributing to overcrowding. This can negatively impact the quality of care. Prolonged wait times are directly associated with "higher risks of mortality, hospital admission, 30-day readmission, patient dissatisfaction, and costs," according to one 2023 report in JAMA.[2]

Another issue is cost. If you have insurance, you can typically get seen at an urgent care clinic for less than $150, which your insurance will cover if you've met your deductible. Your ER costs will always be much higher— maybe even *six times as high*[3]—as what you would pay at an urgent care center. In fact, paying out-of-pocket for an urgent care appointment can be cheaper than your co-pay for an ER visit even if you have insurance, especially if an ambulance is involved. Plus, if too many people are trying to use the ER who shouldn't be there, the overall cost skyrockets for everyone because of that pesky "supply and demand" truism.

• • •

The question of why so many people rush to the ER instead of waiting to see their primary care providers or going to an urgent care clinic is complex, but the underlying problem is usually a lack of access. For instance, some patients may seek out treatment in a hospital ER because they have no insurance or no primary care provider, and most emergency rooms won't turn them away.

"People often have a logical reason for coming to the ER," says Dr. Judd Hollander. This is true even for people who do have insurance, he added.

"Maybe they couldn't get a doctor's appointment in the near future and couldn't find another way to get an evaluation," he says. "Or maybe they couldn't take time off work or find childcare during the day and had to see someone at night. But, let's face it, people go to the ER a) when they have acute injuries, b) when their doctors are unavailable, or c) if they feel they need to be seen right away. Overall, I think the majority of patients who come to the

ER are there because they're uncertain about whether they do or don't have a major problem."

People also know they can get blood tests, imaging, or prescription medications through the ER right away, rather than having to wait for an appointment with their primary care provider or a specialist and have them order these things.

"The ER has become the big box retailer of healthcare," Hollander says. "It's the best one-stop healthcare shopping around."

Marnie's View on Emergency Rooms

As someone who doesn't suffer from illness anxiety, the ER is the last place I want to be. It's a place fraught with injuries and crowded with parked gurneys attached to annoying sounds of beeping. Painful groans make me wince. It's the place that handles the acute, big, scary stuff. If you don't have a concierge medicine plan—which I don't—but you need to see a doctor, it can also be the most frustrating place to be in the middle of the night. Or any other time, for that matter.

Once, for instance, I had to take my daughter, then only two weeks old, to the ER with a high fever. My husband had to stay with our sons, who were only three and four years old at the time, so I asked my mother to meet me at the

Children's Hospital of Philadelphia. (Everyone around here fondly, though perhaps unwisely, abbreviates this hospital's name as "CHOP.") Because it's a teaching hospital, the tendency at CHOP is to run every test imaginable, and they did that on my teeny eight-pound daughter.

Sometimes I feel that having esteemed hospital systems like Penn Medicine (University of Pennsylvania), Children's Hospital of Philadelphia (CHOP), and Jefferson Health makes us Philadelphians the luckiest people in the world—such brilliant minds caring for our every need. Other times, I sort of feel like an experiment or a lesson.

This was one of those times. We arrived at 8 p.m., and three hours later it was already the longest night I'd ever experienced. Finally, the head of the ER popped into the glass-walled waiting room and said, "I want to talk to you about one more test we can run, okay?"

I was eager to know what was happening to my baby, but when I heard the words "lumbar puncture," I nearly passed out with fright. "You want to do a spinal tap? Why?"

"It's to be sure the fever isn't from an infection in the fluid that surrounds her brain or spine," the doctor explained.

My heart raced as the doctor answered my questions about risks during the procedure. My daughter could end up with nerve damage, she could bleed, or she might be in severe pain afterward. I hesitated, not wanting to make this terrible decision. I was overcome with nausea.

My mother snapped me out of it, saying, "Do it. The benefit of knowing far outweighs the risks."

I knew she was right, but what if it was really bad?

The doctor said, "Your daughter has a fever. It could be meningitis. If it is and we treat it, her chances of survival are still just 60 percent. But we have to treat her as soon as possible."

And so, they tapped my baby's spine for fluid, which showed up as normal. The doctor returned with this final diagnosis: "She has a fever of unknown origin. Sometimes that happens. Follow up with your pediatrician."

To me, that's the world of emergency room medicine. It's a place where they test for all the big, scary stuff, even though the odds are that it is none of the serious illnesses. Still, I wouldn't change a thing about that night, because my baby made it.

• • •

A recent study found that "in the United States, approximately 13% to 27% of ER visits can be addressed in ambulatory settings (including urgent care centers). Diverting these patients to the appropriate setting for care could decrease healthcare costs by $4.4 billion."[4] Slowing down the mad rush to emergency departments by people with low-acuity problems—or, as in my case, with health crises that are most likely in our own minds—is key if we're going to stem the rising cost of healthcare. But how can we get more patients to get their complaints treated in more cost-effective settings, like urgent care centers?

We can learn something from Providence, Rhode Island, where an innovative, federally qualified health center facility called Providence Community Health Centers successfully executed a program to prevent avoidable ER visits. They freed up the EMS system to respond to true emergencies and life-threatening conditions by using their Mobile Health Unit to redirect nonemergency 911 callers to urgent care centers. During the twenty-six weeks of the Mobile Health Unit Diversion program under study, 8.4 out of every 10 patients who called 911 and were sent to an urgent care center were discharged home after treatment, avoiding a trip to the ER.[5]

Easing the burden on our country's emergency rooms could very well put us on the path to more effective, efficient patient care for everyone—including hypochondriacs. Accurate ER triage is essential if hospitals are going to devote their resources to providing top-quality care to the most critically ill patients. The most commonly used triage system in the U.S. is the Emergency Severity Index (ESI). This algorithm allows care providers to sort patients based on predicted acuity and resource needs. For instance, Level 1 patients need immediate care, Levels 2 or 3 need care within fifteen minutes, and Levels 4 or 5 require care within thirty minutes.

Currently, mis-triage (inappropriate care) happens nearly a third of the time—often when the emergency room is backed up or short-staffed.[6] Not surprisingly, this occurs most often in poorer neighborhoods, where emergency rooms are more crowded, people are less likely to have private insurance, and many more patients crowd into the ER during nights and weekends.

Triage clinicians are often pressed for time. When that happens, they must make assignments with limited information, because there's no time to truly get to know the patients' histories.

Now let's throw patients with illness anxiety disorder into the mix. When patients with medically unexplained physical symptoms (MUPS) arrive in the ER, clinicians are often stumped. This happens a lot, because MUPS patients comprise up to a third of all those seen in hospital outpatient clinics. In one landmark study of medical outpatients in North America with new complaints of common symptoms like chest pain, dizziness, and headaches, only 16 percent of the cases were found to have an organic cause.[7]

This "somatization" of physical symptoms without any organic explanation is a manifestation of psychological distress—but feels all too real to the person experiencing it. Understandably, most physicians are trained to look for something physically wrong. Meanwhile, there's a growing tendency in emergency medicine toward quickly ruling out the big, scary conditions such as ischemic heart disease, pulmonary embolism, and deep vein thrombosis, among others. Patients who would otherwise wait several weeks for outpatient stress tests can complete assessments in the ER within hours. But this kind of testing is extremely costly, as we'll see in Chapter 11.

Unfortunately, frequent flyers through the healthcare system like Hal might go to the ER again and again to ease uncertainties about this or that pain, and because they rarely see the same providers there, they continue to get testing and referrals to specialists. One solution to this is to ensure that historical records of past ER visits are readily available whenever these cases show up, and to have senior staff confer with junior staff about how to manage patients with chronic somatization by sending them to a primary care provider.

CHAPTER TEN

The Doctor Will See You Now . . . and Any Other Time You Want

Cancer is never far from my mind. Not because I have it, or have *ever* had it, but because I know cancer can kill you. I need all the reassurances I can get, so I'm eternally grateful for my internist, Dr. Matthew J. Killion, MD, my miracle doctor.

During one recent visit, Dr. Killion greeted me with a chirpy, "What's up, Hal? How are you feeling?"

Already I felt better, just seeing him in front of me. "I feel great."

He smiled. "Okay, so why are you here?"

"My wife says I look like I have cancer because I'm too thin."

"Huh." His voice was still cheerful. "You look fine to me, but let's check your weight."

Dr. Killion put me on the scale—naturally, I'd already weighed myself at home, but I never trust my scale like I trust his—and it turned out I'd lost five pounds.

This was to be expected, since I was taking Mounjaro, a

relatively new drug, to treat my type 2 diabetes. Although at the time of this writing Mounjaro hadn't yet been approved for weight loss, there is some evidence that it works even better for that purpose than Ozempic and Wegovy. Clinical trials were fast-tracked for this drug and have already shown that people with elevated body mass indexes (BMIs), but who don't have diabetes, lost weight when taking it.[1]

After Dr. Killion checked my EKG, blood pressure, and lymph nodes, he said, "Take some deep breaths for me now, Hal," as he palpated my chest and back while he listened with his stethoscope.

I'd recently knocked down a sausage sandwich with onions from my favorite street vendor, figuring I'd have to change my diet after seeing him. Exhaling after my first deep breath nearly knocked Dr. Killion back against the wall, and I could see him thinking about double-masking before my next deep breath.

"Everything seems to be in order," he said with a beautiful bedside-manner smile. "Tell me again why you're here."

I asked for a complete blood panel to check for everything under the sun. Fortunately, Dr. Killion draws blood in his office and has it picked up daily. I knew the results would be sent directly to both of us the very next day.

The blood tests, too, showed there was nothing out of the ordinary. Par for the course.

Maybe you're reading this and thinking, "Wow, how

did Hal ever find such a great doctor, one who sees him any time he wants, and really listens to him?"

Partly, it's because I got lucky. When my previous primary care physician, who'd probably had enough with his cadre of patients, which included Harry, fled for the mountains of Colorado, he turned his patients over to my superstar internist. Dr. Killion basically inherited me.

But the real reason I have this kind of top-quality, accessible care is because I'm willing and able to pay for concierge medicine.

Imagine a realm where your every sniffle, pimple, or pain is met with unwavering attention and instant validation or reassurances. With concierge medicine, that panic-inducing paper cut will send your dedicated doctor rushing to your side with a Band-Aid as if it's a matter of life or death.

Concierge doctors will see you on the same day; they are an answer to those in need of immediate gratification. They will also help arrange a drop-in appointment with a specialist, depending on your current complaints. Concierge medicine is expensive, but most people are more willing to pay a premium price for their cell phone and cable bills each month than for a doctor or demand service.

However, concierge medicine is a godsend for hypo-chondriacs. It's a place where the worried well can seek immediate answers and reassurances, but it comes at a hefty price tag.

• • •

Health insurance has been part of our lives since the 1930s. In the 1990s, certain doctors were dissatisfied with the financial coverage they were receiving for services through insurance companies and lamented the increasing pressure they felt to fit more patients into less time. They were frustrated enough to try a new model of care. This practice model is called direct primary care (DPC) and is exactly what it sounds like: patients pay monthly retainer fees in exchange for direct care, such as more accessibility to the doctor through more frequent visits, and even visits outside regular business hours. Such practices may also include discounted lab work or prescriptions.[2]

Concierge medicine is similar to DPC practice, in that both function on a retainer model in exchange for contractual services. However, there's a big difference: DPC practitioners don't bill patient insurance, while concierge physicians still work in tandem with certain insurers.

Dr. Killion never imagined that he'd be offering concierge medicine. However, scarcely six months after starting his own practice and leaving Thomas Jefferson Hospital in Philadelphia, with which he remains affiliated, he reached a grim realization: "I was going broke."

He thought he'd done everything right. After graduating from medical school, he completed an intensive residency in internal medicine and worked in academic medicine for three years. When he went into private practice, he realized certain insurers weren't paying him enough to cover the care he was providing to patients. "I made a decision," he said. "I cut out the HMOs."

That's where he ran into another snag. "When you cut out the HMOs, Independence Blue Cross decreases what they pay you. It's not fair, but they can do that because they're the 800-pound gorilla in Philadelphia."

Dr. Killion had medical school loans, a mortgage, and a child on the way. Recognizing he'd never be able to cover his costs with this business model, "I kicked out all of the insurances but Medicare and went old school, fee-for-service." Patients who wanted to see him were billed directly for any services that weren't covered by Medicare.

His practice flourished. Within a couple of years, he'd built up a nice patient roster and was making a profit. Then, in 2002, one of his patients brought him a newspaper article about concierge medicine, a new healthcare model in which patients paid monthly fees to their physicians. In exchange, these retainer-based physicians would offer services such as guaranteed same-day or next-day appointments, as many appointments as you might want in any given month, more flexible scheduling, access to the doctor's cell phone, and coverage for certain basic services including laboratory testing.

"When my patient told me I should offer concierge

medicine, I just laughed and asked if he was volunteering to be the first one to sign up," Dr. Killion said.

The patient said yes, so Dr. Killion gave the idea some serious thought. "There was no template for concierge medicine at that time," he said. "I would be the first one in Philadelphia to offer it."

Dr. Killion decided to test out a pilot program. After working out a contract with an attorney who specialized in healthcare law, he sent letters to one hundred patients he thought might be interested in this "optional" program. He was shocked when sixty of them signed up right away.

"I thought, 'Okay, this might work,'" he said.

It has. Today, Dr. Killion has about 330 patients, and his reasons for staying with the concierge medicine business model are the same reasons that motivated him to try it in the first place: "I can spend more time with each patient, offer them the best care possible, make a decent living, and have a better work-life balance so I can spend more time with my family."

Whether Dr. Killion's patients see him once a year, a half dozen times, or many more times a year (like me), the annual retainer fee stays the same. For that fee, you get all of the EKGs and lab draws your heart desires. Believe me, my heart has desired those things more times than I can count.

As Dr. Killion told me with a laugh, "It's true that I lose money on some patients. But, overall, it works out."

• • •

In 2022, the concierge medicine market in this country was valued at $6.1 billion, and the expectation is that it will grow at a compound annual rate of over 10 percent by 2030.[3]

Why would this be so? One reason is accessibility. According to the newest data from the Association of American Medical Colleges, the United States may experience an estimated shortage of up to 124,000 physicians by 2034.[4]

We're already feeling the pinch. Researchers point out that the average wait time for a patient to schedule an appointment with a new doctor has increased 8 percent since 2017. This isn't true for concierge medicine, where doctors offer immediate appointments. They also spend more time with their patients since their patient load is less.[5]

Our population is aging fast, and there will be higher and higher demands for primary care services in the near future. This increases the work burden on these doctors, who already aren't being compensated well enough for what they do, according to Dr. Killion.

"The entire medical reimbursement system has shifted toward procedure-based specialties like dermatology or orthopedists," he said. "If you ask why there's a shortage in primary care, consider looking at the disgruntled doctors who are asking why they should bust their asses for sixty or even ninety hours a week, but still make only a tenth of what specialists make. The healthcare system itself caused the problem."

. . .

Naturally many people—including me—recognize that concierge medicine is just one more example of the enormous divide between the haves and have-nots in our country. It's a little bit like going to Disneyland and seeing all those people waiting in line, while certain families can afford the fast pass and jump to the front. Or like watching certain people settle into first-class seats on a plane while others are herded into coach, where there are no meals, and their knees bump up against the seat in front of them.

Concierge medicine is the domain of people with money. Each concierge doctor charges a different rate, but I conjecture that most range from $2,500 to $5,000 annually. My own cost is $3,000 annually.

The irony here is that, while that's a lot of money, the savings for the healthcare system for someone like me are tremendous, since I'm not running up the emergency room bills when nothing is really wrong in the first place. For my peace of mind, it's worth every penny.

And, while there's a shortage of primary care doctors, and some might argue that concierge medicine sucks even more physicians out of the system, it's also true that concierge medicine is typically used by the "worried well."

Bottom line: we're not taking up space or time in the ER or urgent clinics, and that benefits everyone.

For instance, I remember a story Harry shared with me about the time he collapsed on the floor of his home and had trouble breathing. Harry's wife, who might have otherwise called for an ambulance, instructed him to call our doctor. (Dr. Killion is Harry's doctor, too.)

After Harry answered several of Dr. Killion's questions regarding what had happened over the last few hours, anxiety set in as he awaited the doctor's prognosis, fearing a seizure or mini-stroke. Finally, Dr. Killion delivered his verdict: he determined that Harry had stuffed his mouth too quickly with Chinese food and had OD'd on chicken with cashews, steamed wontons, and Dan Dan noodles. "Chew slower," was Dr. Killion's sage prescription.

Harry hasn't fainted since. He now enjoys wonton soup sans dumplings.

Now, compare that with the costs that would have been incurred by Harry, the healthcare system, and Harry's insurance company if he'd been rushed to the hospital, where they would have run numerous tests only to find chicken with cashews, six pork dumplings, and a bowl of noodles as the cause of his symptoms and distress.

Most recently, Harry has been experiencing bowel

problems, hitting the head often but unable to produce a solid stool for months at a time. Our friend Stan, the third member of The Boys Club, suggested that Harry try eating a pickle, made without vinegar, each morning.

"That solved the problem for me," Stan assured Harry.

Harry rushed over to Hymie's delicatessen and headed for the pickle bar, where he asked the server if the pickles were made with vinegar.

The clerk gave him a bewildered look, clearly thinking, *How else do you think they make pickles?*

Undeterred, Harry grabbed a bunch of pickles and headed to the register, where he added a pound cake and a dozen schnecken to get rid of the pickle taste.

For weeks, Harry chomped down a pickle each morning to no avail. Finally, after some hesitation because he'd already contacted him twice that same day, Harry called Dr. Killion.

"My friend Stan suggested that eating one pickle daily will cure my inconvenient loose waste problem," he said, "so I went to Hymie's and loaded up on pickles. I've been eating one a day but it's not working. What do you think?"

"I think pickles go great with corned beef sandwiches," Dr. Killion said, and set up an appointment with a GI specialist.

This time, Harry knew his issue was a real one. Maybe he wasn't completely crazy after all.

CHAPTER ELEVEN

I Want That Test, Too!

Early one morning, Harry called to say he was suffering from horrendously painful cramps on both sides of his abdomen.

"This time I thought it might just be constipation, but when I pulled down my pants, I saw a huge bulge to the left of my penis!" Harry whispered into the phone, sounding horrified.

He went on to share even more gory details. I listened patiently, knowing that Harry suffers even more from illness anxiety than I do.

"I stood in front of the mirror and thought, *What if I have testicular cancer?*" Harry moaned. "What if this is really it, Hal?"

Harry has been terrified of having cancer ever since his own father died of pancreatic cancer. He is rarely satisfied by the variety of reassuring responses he receives from his friends, family, coworkers, neighbors, and, to a certain degree, Stan and me. Before calling me that morning, Harry had already launched his typical grand-scale investigation of lumps on Google. Doubled over in pain, he stared at his phone, reading the zillion hits he'd gotten while searching for his symptoms and hoping to eliminate cancer. Harry settled on spermatic cord pain and became overwhelmed with paranoia that one of his testicles would need to be removed, as described in an article written by the Urology Care Foundation.

"Is it true?" he kept whispering as he frantically scrolled through his phone, diving deeper into WebMD, Zocdoc, Healthline, and the Mayo Clinic websites.

After ninety minutes of high anxiety, he called our concierge doctor once again. Harry was the first in our friend group to hop on the concierge bandwagon with me. In the social circles of hypochondriacs in suburban Philadelphia, the $3,000 per year we pay for this service is a pittance in return for same-day appointments.

"Think of it as having that black card issued to American Express Elite Centurion members," I had told Harry. "We're the frequent flyers of the healthcare system, only instead of hanging out in the Admirals Club at airports, we're strutting through the corridors of our local hospital, flexing at the reception desk."

So, as Harry described it to me later, at 7 a.m. on a Saturday, he called Dr. Killion and stammered shamelessly on about his latest calamity, starting with, "The bulge is to the left of my penis."

"Send me a picture, Harry," Dr. Killion replied through a stifled yawn. "I'll call you right back."

Harry strained to take a good selfie of the bulge and sent it off. Thirty seconds later, Dr. Killion called to say, "I've got some bad news for you, Harry."

Harry's heart rate doubled and his vision tunneled. "What is it?"

After a pause, Dr. Killion chuckled and said, "Porn really isn't your strong suit. You need to stick to selling insurance."

Harry, barely able to recover from the phrase "bad news," hardly heard the doctor say he thought it might be a hernia but wouldn't know for sure until his office opened on Monday and he could check him out in person.

"But it's not cancer," Dr. Killion added in a soothing voice.

Somewhat relieved, but completely apoplectic at the idea of having to endure two more days of worrying, Harry hung up. Afraid to tell his wife, who already considers him a nutcase when it comes to health issues, he dropped his drawers to take one more look.

To his amazement, the bulge was gone! Had he imagined it?

During Harry's appointment on Monday, Dr. Killion couldn't locate a bulge, but suggested an ultrasound to rule out a hernia. The physician at the hospital couldn't find a bulge, either, but proceeded with the ultrasound.

After the test, the attending physician said, "It's not a hernia, Harry."

Harry experienced a moment of blessed relief before the doctor added, "There might be a problem with the spermatic cord. I'd suggest you get a colonoscopy to make sure nothing else is causing your cramps," which brought back memories of the research Harry had performed online suggesting the cure was to cut off a testicle.

• • •

After worrying for three days that he might have multiple issues, Harry had the colonoscopy. The results showed nothing to worry about, but the colon guy suggested an endoscopy to see what else might be causing the cramps. "You've got a cyst on your kidney that has doubled in size," he noted.

Meanwhile, a hundred miles away, Harry's son was experiencing the same sort of cramps. Harry insisted that he go to a clinic for an exam, where his son was told he had shingles at age thirty. This news threw a whole new twist into the scary plot developing in Harry's head. He immediately phoned Dr. Killion to apprise him of the latest development.

A couple of days later, Harry had a follow-up with Dr. Killion, who revealed that the spermatic cord issue, which Harry was worrying would necessitate the removal of at least one testicle, wasn't the issue.

"I'm still convinced that the pic you sent points to a hernia," he said. "That ultrasound wasn't conclusive. I'm going to refer you to the most well-respected hernia expert I know."

A meeting with this doctor confirmed that Harry did, indeed, probably have a hernia. After a day of apparent relief—*it's not cancer!*—Harry's mind spun out of control again. He was convinced the surgeon wouldn't find a hernia, but rather something else they hadn't even considered yet! He was thrown into a state of perpetual anxiety as he awaited his fate.

Unfortunately, two weeks later his original cramps reappeared in the same area of his abdomen. Fearing that Dr. Killion would think he was a hypochondriac, Harry decided not to call, but rather gut it out and see what happened. A month passed, during which he reconsidered his plan and returned to the hospital for another ultrasound. This time the imaging showed that the suspected hernia seemed to have miraculously disappeared along with the cramps.

Not to be consoled by too much good news, Harry scheduled an appointment with a gastroenterologist to find out what else might be going on. This guy didn't find anything, either. Harry's anxiety took a brief vacation until a severe headache persisted for days and his mind turned to a potential brain tumor. He was too afraid to call Dr. Killion again, as alarms might go off in his office when caller ID recognized who the incoming call was from.

A previously scheduled visit with his dentist showed that Harry had an infected wisdom tooth. He returned a few days later to have it treated by an endodontist; rather than having the tooth removed, he opted to have them drain the infection.

A couple of days later, Harry's cramps reappeared, probably as a result of swallowing the infection during the procedure to drain it. He returned to Dr. Killion for advice. "I'm really afraid of how this might be affecting my organs," he said.

Dr. Killion prescribed an antibiotic to kill the infection, and Harry returned to his state of constant anxiety, despite no doctor being able to find anything related to his bulge, cramps, or brain tumor.

Finally, when Harry heard that a new company in Florida was offering a powerful full-body MRI for a price, he paid to have it done, and was told there was absolutely nothing wrong with him.

By now, I suspected Dr. Killion was probably going into spasms each time one of us called. This time it was me.

"I've been having a lot of headaches lately. I might have

a brain tumor," I told Dr. Killion the next time we spoke. "What would you think of me getting a full-body and brain scan to rule that out?"

"You don't need it," he said. "It's a waste of money, Hal."

As usual, Dr. Killion was correct. Given my state of health, it wasn't worth the time or money, as an article in the *Wall Street Journal* confirmed recently, citing that the demand for preventive scans for seemingly healthy patients has surged. The scans can be costly, too, as the article notes, since follow-ups can lead to more unnecessary costs and procedures that might cause complications.[1]

While I trust Dr. Killion implicitly, I also knew Harry had a scan and was relieved when they found nothing. Now I wanted a scan, too, not for medical reasons, but for emotional ones.

• • •

At the height of my worries about cancer hiding "somewhere" in my body and brain, I scheduled a PET-MRI scan of both. I knew it would be expensive, but living with the unknown was debilitating.

It took months for me to get an appointment. While I waited for the date to approach, my emotions ping-ponged between best- and worst-case scenarios. *Wouldn't it be great if they found nothing, and I didn't need to worry about cancer for at least a year*, I thought. Or, alternatively, I was convinced I was about to be handed a death sentence.

I also started listing all the symptoms I'd been experiencing over the years and the questions I wanted to ask when I arrived for the scan. This meant paying greater attention to any newly advertised drugs and any signs that I might have the diseases targeted by the commercials on TV.

Did I have early signs of Alzheimer's disease, which had been suggested by my wife? No. How about colon cancer? No. Was I experiencing early signs of rheumatoid arthritis? Maybe. Shingles? Had I ever had chicken pox? No idea. My memory didn't go back that far, and my mother, then ninety-three years old, couldn't help either.

When the day came, I entered the Integrative Medicine Center for the scan, where I was first infused with a liquid the technician took from what looked like a lead box resembling the "nuclear football."

After thirty minutes of waiting for my radioactive body to resemble a walking Chernobyl, I was led into the newest version of a PET-MRI scanning machine. My body was spun back into the Tunnel of Tumors, and after ten minutes of banging noises, the technician interrupted me as I was trying to relax by struggling to remember my football chants from high school.

"I'm afraid the machine has broken down for the first time ever," the technician said. "We'll have to get you out of there, Hal."

They slid me out and asked me to go back into the room designed for me to "rest my brain" while they tried to reboot the machine. Half an hour crawled by before the doctor came in to say he was headed up to the roof, where he hoped to look at the coolant system.

"That might be what brought the machine down," he said. "It might have overheated."

"Might have?" I asked, but he was already gone.

The doctor reappeared eventually, soaking wet from playing plumber. "I think I might have solved the problem, but why don't you just stay here and relax in the dark while we reboot for the second time? Shouldn't be more than fifteen minutes."

My brain was now in full explosion mode as I became convinced that the scan would produce something from all the anxiety I was experiencing, if nothing else.

At long last, the technician returned to the "relaxation room" and said, "Okay, it's time."

I walked back to the scanning room just as the machine broke down again. This time I insisted on staying to watch the newest rebooting effort and noticed that the computer used to perform the reboot was a Microsoft Windows 7 version released in 2009. Now my pulse hammered. It was 2022! Why weren't they using Windows 11?

After yet more fiddling, it was time for me to be launched by NASA. At T-minus one minute, I was instructed to climb back into the scanner. Twenty minutes later, my brain scan was complete. The next forty minutes would be spent imaging my body.

At that point, I hadn't eaten in eighteen hours and my nose had an itch I couldn't scratch. All I could think about was getting out of there, scratching my nose, and reentering the earth's atmosphere.

When the scan was complete, I was led back to the relaxation room while the doctor read my results. Relax, my ass. I was now attempting slow, rhythmic breathing, as if I were about to give birth.

When the doctor returned, it was to say that the results from Windows 7 were slow.

No news flash there, I thought.

"Come on back with me and we can read the results together in real time," he said.

If you do that, you won't have any time to think about how you're going to gently break the bad news to me, I thought, but I went back with him anyway.

We started with the brain scan. My frontal lobes were glowing on the images. I was ready to pass out with terror at the sight.

"Oh, don't worry about that," the doctor said. "That's probably just from your anxiety caused by the scanner breaking down."

Okay, we were off to a pretty good start. He showed me that the rest of my brain was fine, "clear of cancer," and that I showed no signs of Alzheimer's disease.

We then switched to my body images, where the first thing I saw was a spot on a lymph node. Mild panic set in, until the doctor asked if I'd recently had a COVID booster in my left arm.

"Yes, three days ago," I said.

"Okay, good to know. We've been seeing these spots lately on people who've had boosters," he said. "They always appear in the lymph node residing under the arm where the shot was administered."

My heart rate subsided. He went through the rest of the results, basically saying, "There's nothing wrong with you."

The doctor was thorough, I'll give him that. He wanted me to stay so he could discuss every image of every organ, but once I had been given the all clear, I was in full retreat to the parking lot, pausing only to ask, "What about my pancreas?"

"It's fine, Hal," he said.

That was good enough for me. I ran out of there to celebrate with a Philly cheese steak.

• • •

Rising healthcare costs in the U.S. have sparked an ongoing dialogue about the value of preventive health—and about what kind of medical testing is actually necessary.

Testing is an essential part of medicine. The volume of medical tests performed in this country is enormous, with up to five billion tests ordered each year across all specialties. Various studies have shown that 40 to 60 percent of tests are unnecessary, and that this can lead to what's called a "diagnostic cascade," in which the unnecessary testing leads to false positive results and to other tests—or even to superfluous medical procedures.[2]

Laboratory testing is healthcare's biggest volume activity, with 14 billion laboratory tests being ordered annually, according to the CDC.[3] Although another blood test or two isn't going to break anybody's bank, the problem lies in what happens next, like the unnecessary additional testing or more medical visits that aren't needed, either.

Most doctors and patients acknowledge there's a lot of unnecessary testing, so why does this continue happening?

Sometimes it's due to patient requests, especially when doctors are faced with challenging patients who suffer from illness anxiety disorder like Harry and me. We're pretty sure we have whatever our minds are telling us we have, and because physicians are schooled to "do no harm" by making sure they rule out every little thing when we're in pain, they order medical testing to reassure us and themselves.

Ideally, physicians offer patients "high-value" care, which means they deliver thorough and appropriate exams, testing, and treatments. But when they start offering "low-value services" like unwarranted blood tests or imaging, that can boost healthcare costs over $300 billion a year. These tests can also cause doctors to make potentially poor decisions if they receive clinically irrelevant test results that trigger a diagnostic cascade.[4]

Various medical societies have been pushing for their members to identify "non-value" tests or procedures commonly used in their fields. For instance, doctors are now encouraged *not* to do imaging studies in patients with low back pain or migraines, and not to bother testing men over eighty for prostate cancer since it's so slow-moving.

Yet, many physicians continue to order unnecessary tests, partly because that's the way they've been trained—many doctors subscribe to the idea that doing something is better than doing nothing. Besides, if they work for a hospital system, the pressure is on for them to offer more tests because that's where the profit lies.

Doctors often also err on the side of over-testing because malpractice lawsuits are always looming over their heads. What if they skip a test and miss something? Why not do the test and be certain?

Using these so-called "defensive medical practices," both physicians and hospitals prevent lawsuits by ensuring that they have documented a certain level of care. They can also give their patients the reassurances they so desperately seek. Much of what doctors do every day is manage patient uncertainty, and testing can give their patients answers and help them relax.

Or maybe not. As Harry and I know too well, we are reassured only momentarily before we move on to our next dire fear.

• • •

As we established earlier in the book, the United States spends more on healthcare than any other high-income country does. Yet we still have the highest rate of people with multiple chronic diseases and some of the worst health outcomes, according to a recent research report by The Commonwealth Fund.[5] Their data showed that, in 2021 alone, the U.S. spent almost twice as much as other countries participating in the Organization for Economic Cooperation and Development (OECD), which tracks and reports on data from health systems from thirty-eight different high-income countries.

As far as testing goes, the U.S. comes out as one of the pricier places to lay your body down inside an MRI tube or make a fist for a blood draw. Lab testing can range from $100 to over $1,000, whether or not you have insurance.[6] Cutting back on unnecessary medical testing could help bring down not only wait times for patients, but healthcare costs.

But I have another, more controversial solution as well: what if we all (especially those of us who suffer from illness anxiety) had better access to *more* medical testing?

People with severe illness anxiety use between 41 and 78 percent more healthcare than other people, which of course raises costs. There's another hidden cost, too: our chronic worrying takes a toll on the body. In one study, "the researchers found that high levels of illness anxiety increased the risk of coronary heart disease by 70 percent." Additionally, "there is some evidence that illness anxiety has an effect on overall mortality rate."[7]

Making full-body scans, ultrasounds, full blood panels, and other kinds of testing more readily available might actually curb our nation's healthcare spending, especially when you consider people with hypochondria. I, for one, felt a lot better after my own full-body scan showed that I had absolutely nothing abnormal going on. This knowledge has kept me from calling Dr. Killion as many times a month as I used to do. I now plan to schedule a full-body scan every two years, just to put my mind at ease at least for a while.

As I've also said before, my ultimate fantasy is to build an exam room in my own basement, complete with an exam table, ultrasound and EKG machine, a high-intensity video set-up, and a technician on call to administer the tests and send them to the appropriate provider. I'd also like to have my own room at the hospital, outfitted the way I'd like it and held empty for me in case I need it, though I'd be happy for others to use it when I'm not in need.

Ironically, while proofreading this chapter I'm sitting in a hospital bed following the insertion of a stent for a 99 percent artery blockage, and scraping the graham cracker crumbs off my gown. The entire staff has been fantastic. However, I would like to have redesigned the room with a wide-screen HD TV, an honor bar, and a Sleep Number bed.

Since none of the above is likely to happen, I'm watching new technologies come down the pike with great interest. For instance, the health tech startup Neko Health, which was co-founded by Spotify co-creator Daniel Ek, raised $65 million in its very first external round of funding. What are they promising? To offer full-body scans backed by AI software that can help physicians detect cancer, diabetes, and heart disease, among other things. The scans would be affordable, too, at around $250 each.[8]

It seems to me that this kind of innovation bodes well not only for hypochondriacs like me who are willing and able to shell out money to give ourselves peace of mind, but for the overburdened healthcare system overall. Making it possible for people to arrange and manage their own medical testing eliminates the problematic middleman of health insurance companies.

I'm a big believer in proactive measures that can help detect potential issues early on and give patients more access to their data, so we can all make more informed health decisions. My own experience with full-body scans has been helpful in assessing my overall health and alleviating any fears I have about chronic conditions I need to manage. I look forward to seeing how more investment in this space will push the technology and processes further along to be more accessible to a wider range of patients.

CHAPTER TWELVE

Horses, Hay, and Hypochondria

For more than thirty-five years, I've spent half my time living and working in suburban Philadelphia and the other half on a ranch in rural North Dakota. Recently, I returned to my house at the ranch after a long day in the fields harvesting hay for my horses and cattle, sat down, popped open a Coors Light, and had this thought: Why do I so rarely experience hypochondriacal thoughts when I'm here?

Since 2019, I have had countless laboratory tests in Philadelphia, as well as twenty-nine visits to the hospital for procedures and ER visits. These have included echocardiography, radiology, cardiology, endocrinology, ultrasounds, CT scans, gastroenterology, hepatology, catheterization, and otolaryngology. Only the cardiology tests showed anything amiss.

Guess how many times I've been to the hospital in North Dakota? Only when I've been kicked by a cow or bucked off by a horse and needed stitches or a cast.

There's the same kind of imbalance in doctors' visits. For instance, not long ago in Philadelphia, my right ear felt clogged. I decided to see if I could clear it out by using cotton swabs, ear wash, and picking at the crust forming inside the ear. When my hearing didn't improve, I finally relented and headed to my internist. He inspected my ear and washed it out.

I felt relief for a few days. Then that dullness reoccurred, and I headed back to the doctor for another look-see. This time I was diagnosed with an ear infection and prescribed an antibiotic.

A week after completing my regimen of twice-daily consumption of the antibiotic, I was hoping for at least some relief. Instead, the pain that had originally been confined to my ear seemed to be moving above and below it. So, off I went to a renowned ENT doctor. He investigated my ear and said he couldn't see anything other than the crust, and there was nothing for me to be concerned about. Nonetheless, I left his office with a potion he'd concocted that blows some kind of powder into my ear, because I'd mentioned that sometimes the daily secretions I was experiencing seemed to be of the wet variety.

"Contact me if that persists," he said.

I headed home and started a daily regimen of blow-drying my ear with this stuff. It seemed to help a bit. However, a week later the crust reappeared, and I made an appointment to return to the ENT. He once again did a thorough exam and saw nothing, so I asked him for a medication that might get rid of the dry crust. He called a prescription for liquid drops into the pharmacy, and that seemed to work.

After a few months, I returned to the ENT, who is a real pro, and was told there was nothing wrong with my ear. He suggested a visit to the audiology department at the hospital to have my hearing checked. That visit cost $400, and I left with a recommendation that I return in three weeks to be fitted for a hearing aid.

Now, contrast that experience with this one: here in North Dakota, I was being kept awake with horrible cramps in my calf. When I mentioned this to my friend Dave, he said, "I always take two spoonfuls of yellow mustard for cramps."

Guess what? I tried it, and it works. Now I just keep a jar of yellow mustard on my bedside table.

So, what's the difference? Why does my illness anxiety always skyrocket in Philadelphia, when the reality is that I'm more likely to get hurt out on the range in North Dakota?

• • •

People often ask me, "How the hell did you end up in North Dakota?"

Truth be known, I ended up with a ranch in North Dakota because of a horrific two-year drought.

The 1988–1989 drought still ranks amongst the worst
in this country, causing billions of dollars in damage and
making it one of the costliest natural disasters in America's
history. A segment on the TV news in Philadelphia about
farmers in North Dakota losing their livestock and ranches
to the drought inspired a sudden brainstorm. At that time,
my travel company was performing data entry from all over
the world, handling literally tens of thousands of clients
from corporations who were booking their employees on
business trips. Why not set up a call center in North Dakota,
one of the places hardest hit by the drought, and hire many
of the farm wives in the county? We could train them on our
company's new technology, and they'd have jobs that might
literally save their farms.

So, after meeting with the governor's team in North
Dakota, we turned a huge, abandoned John Deere center
that had a concrete floor and a wood-burning stove into a
data and call center. The townspeople gave us chairs, and
the church gave us tables. We brought in the computers and
started training the farmers' wives on them. We started small
at first, with forty women, but eventually ended up with
around two hundred employees in a town of 1,500 people.

One day, one of the women I'd hired said, "Would you
like to come out and have lunch at my ranch?"

"Sure," I said. I was visiting from Philadelphia and
hadn't really seen much of the countryside at that point.

Once we were on the ranch, her husband, Dave, invited me out to the barn to see his cows. I grew up in the city, so the only cow I'd ever seen before was the token cow at the Philadelphia Zoo. Dave brought me out into the cow pens, and of course I was like Billy Crystal in *City Slickers*, sinking into the spring muck (and worse) in my urban khakis and loafers.

"What do you think of my cows?" Dave asked, eyeing my shoes, which were now pretty much buried from sight.

I kept a straight face and said, "I think they're lovely."

He must have thought I was nuts, and I couldn't blame him.

The next year, I drove out to visit Dave again after stopping at the call center to see how everyone was doing. He gave me a horse and we rode out into the fields to find any cows that might be in trouble. I'd taken riding lessons in Philadelphia, and had even done a little jumping, but riding in a ring or an arena was nothing like riding across the open plains. It felt like flying.

Sure enough, we found a cow giving birth, and she was in trouble. When Dave dismounted and got down on his knees to help out, I asked why he wasn't calling the vet.

He shook his head. "That would cost money. We only call the vet if things look critical and I don't have the means of helping her. Besides, the nearest one is thirty-five miles away."

Dave took out his rope, put his hand inside the cow, tied the rope around the calf's ankles, and pulled. Out came the calf! I'd seldom seen anything as profoundly moving.

• • •

Our travel company went on to open four more call centers in the state over the next few years, eventually employing a couple of thousand people. I found I liked doing business in North Dakota, where pretty much every deal was done over a handshake. One day, I asked a realtor in town if he could find me some land, since I was spending so much time out there and found it both exhilarating and calming.

When he did, I was already back in Philadelphia. "You'd better hurry up and come out here," he said. "It's a nice piece of land and there's lots of interest."

I went back to North Dakota in the dead of winter, in a whiteout blizzard, and looked at this land. "What's out there?" I asked the realtor. "I can't see a thing."

"The Missouri River and rolling hills," he said. "Great land for cattle."

We shook hands and I bought the land not even knowing what it looked like. Next, with Dave's help, I bought a hundred head of cattle and started my small herd. Then I built an executive retreat out there with eighteen rooms. I brought in a chef from the Sonoma Mission Inn and worked with the Ritz-Carlton organization to train people to work there.

Shortly thereafter, I created oxymoronic events, holding black-tie-and-boots cattle drives with the CEOs we were courting for business. I brought in lots of media personalities from the major networks to help draw them to North Dakota, which I've heard called "a state to drive through to get to another."

We taught our corporate clients how to ride and gave leadership conferences where the guest speakers would talk for an hour, then walk down to the stable with the rest of the guests to head out for a trail ride. If I wanted to acquire a company, I'd invite executives out of the formal boardroom and into the rocking chairs outside on the porch.

I remember once sitting in my family room with a bevy of Walgreens executives who were beating around the bush on a potential acquiree and avoiding the big question. I was getting bored. Wasting time out here is a big no-no. Finally, I spoke up and asked the chairman of the targeted public company if he wanted to jump on a horse and ride with me up to the top of one of my bluffs.

Once we got to the top of the hill, we rested our horses and I asked, "Want to sell your company?" He answered yes, I asked how much, and he replied between $3 and $5 a share.

I replied, "Deal. If it's worth $3, you get $3, and after

due diligence, if it's worth $4 or $5, you get that." That's the Cowboy Way: get to the point, use common sense, and get it done.

It should have been stressful, doing so much business, but it never was. I learned from my cowboy friends, and from being under that big sky with the animals, that you can't control everything, so why try? No stress, no anxiety, no hypochondria.

I created an office inside my tractor by installing a couple of computers, so that I could be online and even answer emails while I'm haying on the ranch. If I have enough reception, I can have a conference or Zoom call. That allows me to be informed while I'm doing monotonous, therapeutic work. I can listen to the radio, too, when I'm out on the tractor. I always listen to the farm reports instead of the news. Then I turn to country music, actually focusing on the words while making round after round of raking up hay.

So, again, where's my hypochondria when I'm on the ranch? Practically nonexistent. Hmm.

A few years ago, for instance, on a hot August day, my neighbor and best childhood friend Joe Sciolla, who, as I mentioned earlier, had followed me out to North Dakota and built a ranch five miles away, was trying to train a two-year-old horse for his daughter, Caitlin.

Joe was riding the young horse in a pen and trying to

get him to break from a trot into a lope, but the colt refused. When I showed up on my motorcycle, Joe was dismounting from the horse, ready to give up for the day.

I was wearing shorts, a tank top, and sneakers—not the ideal outfit for riding, if you think you might end up on the ground—but, when Joe explained the situation, I said, "I'll get him to lope."

"Dad, you're not going to let Hal ride my horse, are you?" Caitlin asked in alarm. "He'll kill himself."

Joe just smiled at me and said, "Sure, Hal. If you want to ride him, he's all yours." (He told me later he was trying hard not to laugh, already knowing what would happen.)

So, I mounted and got the colt to start walking a little. Then I widened my legs and kicked the horse. The horse stopped dead, and I fanned him again with my heels.

Later, Joe said it was like the animal had a caption coming out of his head, saying, "This son of a bitch just fanned me!"

"Dad," Caitlin said, "make Hal get off the horse!"

But Joe just kept smiling while the colt rolled his eyes and bucked me off, launching me like a missile. For about three seconds after I landed, I was perfectly balanced on my head and shoulders. Then I went over like a tree. When I stood up it was like I'd been tarred, because the sand stuck to my sweaty skin—and I knew I'd broken yet more ribs.

Joe is now an expert rider and trainer, although his last

self-imposed horse accident landed him in the hospital. A medical helicopter touched down in my fields and proceeded to fly him to Bismarck, where he surpassed my twelve broken ribs with a new winning total of twenty. I was pissed about this, since Joe has typically beaten me in pretty much everything since we were eight years old and first started playing Wiffle ball almost daily in Elkins Park, Pennsylvania, which we continued to do until we were eighteen, becoming inseparable friends in the process.

Out here on the ranch, the antidote for anxiety-ridden health fantasies is fixing tractors, pulling calves, breaking horses, and figuring out how not to get injured doing so. I have not always been successful in that last quest, having been busted up mostly from being rammed by cows and dumped by young horses.

But I'm never sick. Nor do I typically worry about being sick or dying out here, unlike in Philadelphia, where my illness anxiety is apt to rear its ugly head anytime and anywhere. There has to be some reason for that. If I could only bottle it up, I'd make millions.

• • •

When I look at how I live in North Dakota and compare it to how I live in Pennsylvania, one of the biggest changes in my lifestyle is that out on the ranch I'm too physically occupied to pay much attention to my ailments, imagined or real. If there's cattle to be moved between fields, the needs of the animals take priority because they can't survive without me. I worry more about the livestock and my friends and forget about myself.

I don't hang around with any hypochondriacs in North Dakota, either. My friends in that part of the country are apt to get together and drink whiskey while we talk about sports and ranching. We seldom talk politics. Nobody's a news junkie, because for years we only got three channels out there. Anyway, there isn't much time to talk about the nonsense going on in other parts of the world and the anxiety it brings.

Unlike my conversations with Harry and Stan in Gladwyne, Pennsylvania, which often center on our medical concerns, my discussions with my cowboy friend and neighbor Dave often take place while sitting on rocking chairs looking out on the prairie, and sound more like this:

"Hal, it's greening up."

"Yup," I reply.

Three minutes later, he'll have a refrain and say, "It's really greening up."

"Yup," I answer, and take another sip of whiskey, feeling thankful for the rain we had recently and wondering when it will rain again.

Half an hour later, Dave turns to me and says, "Looks

like it's clouding up."

"Yup, seems like it's closing in."

"Say, Hal, do you have time to help me round up a few of my horses that broke through one of my fences before it storms?"

"Yup, let's do it," I answer.

As we wrap up our day, the conversation typically turns to how much we accomplished together and what's in store for tomorrow.

Whenever I do mention something like, "I've got this headache. I think I might have a migraine," when I'm out riding with Joe, he'll shrug and say, "You're probably just getting dehydrated. Drink some water."

In Philadelphia, there's another difference, too: healthcare concerns are constantly in my face. I'm constantly driving by hospitals, urgent care centers, and pharmacy clinics. I'm bombarded by Big Pharma commercials on TV and billboards along the highway. And, because my business revolves around healthcare, my mind and inbox are crammed with thoughts and ideas related to diseases and the rising prevalence of anxiety and depression in America.

Out on the ranch, there are very few structures in sight. It's a big sunrise in the morning and a big sunset at night. The closest hospital and pharmacy are more than thirty miles away. There are no billboards, urgent care signs, or other subliminal signals that I should get that blood test again or have a second opinion on the migraines I was experiencing.

In addition, rather than immersing myself in the local and national TV stations I watch back in Pennsylvania, in North Dakota I make it a point to only watch the BBC, which never airs any Pharma commercials. Or I turn to the ME channel, where I watch reruns of *Leave It to Beaver, Wagon Train,* and *Gunsmoke.* Otherwise, I'm checking a Bismarck station now and then to see what the weather's doing. Unlike Philadelphia, the only shootings on the local news are typically relegated to deer season.

Is that the secret to my feeling well? The fact that I'm out of the city and both busier and more relaxed?

As Joe said once while we were enjoying martinis on his porch at sunset, "We're actors in the theater of the absurd. Out here it plays better to just enjoy life."

• • •

Scientific studies show that humans have an infinite capacity to learn and retain information. As a CEO, author, and busy family man with adult children, I'm constantly having new information and ideas deposited into my brain—so much of it that I feel the need to purge information now and then to create room for new knowledge.

The only thing I really worry about out here is the weather. In the summer, ranchers face the fear of an elongated dry spell that often leads to a drought. Tornadoes, hail, and wild winds can wreak havoc on our land, barns, homes, and livestock. The winter brings on a different worry as blizzards transform the prairie into a white expanse. Calving season means keeping an eye out for cows birthing in a whiteout and the resultant loss of newborn calves. In every case, we need to jump into action and quickly tend to our ranches and livestock regardless of the extreme weather conditions.

Most mornings, though, I carry a cup of coffee out to the back porch and gaze over the prairie before starting my day. It's a slice of heaven on earth.

While I have plenty of time to think in my tractor out in the fields, I tend to let my mind wander, and luckily it usually goes nowhere. When checking cows on my horse, the thing that holds my attention is trying to avoid gopher holes and being tossed skyward. In other words, it's harder work out here, but a blessedly simpler existence.

CHAPTER THIRTEEN

Wearing My Health on My Sleeve

A lot of classic literature—and I'm not even talking hardcore sci-fi here—predicted the kind of medical technology we regularly use today. For instance, Mary Shelley's *Frankenstein,* published in 1818, foreshadowed the development of everything from bioelectronics and genetic engineering to organ transplants and AI.

I'm not blessed with that kind of prescient imagination, but it's clear to me that wearable healthcare technology is quickly transforming the way we'll maintain our health in the future. That's both a blessing and a curse for hypochondriacs.

The good news is that this technology is leading us to a place in which healthcare will be more accessible and a lot cheaper. The bad news is that those of us with illness anxiety might have even more things to worry about, like whether our technology is failing, what that graph on our phone screen really means, and who has access to our medical records.

So what, exactly, is wearable health technology?

It's two steps into the future from information technology.

• • •

We've already embraced information technology. I'm betting you're already using your phone to bank online, make restaurant reservations, tip your hair stylist, and play games. You may even be using wearable technology, that broad category of smart electronic products incorporated into accessories that can be attached to your body. These include the Fitbit, Samsung Gear, and Apple Watch.

These gadgets are part of a broad category researchers call the "Internet of Things" (IoT). (Seriously, you'd think the people who invent these things, as brilliant as they are, could come up with a better name.) Wearable healthcare technology is any smart electronic product that can be attached to our bodies to help us continually monitor our physiological parameters and overall health. We can even use it to share data with our healthcare providers. On a very basic level, for instance, many people rely on a Fitbit or Apple Watch synced with their phone to track how many steps they've walked or how many calories they've consumed.

Developers are continuing to create and test innovative new healthcare wearable technology devices. For instance, MIT researchers have designed an ultrasound device that can be attached to a bra for the purpose of detecting early stages of breast cancer.[1] Another group of engineers from the University of California, San Diego, has successfully created what they describe as an "entirely integrated wearable ultrasound system for deep-tissue tracking."[2] This kind of device might one day serve to monitor cardiovascular health, since it can wirelessly sense vital signs in deep tissue.

This is all great news, right? I mean, why not go ahead and develop a jock strap to detect testicular cancer, too?

Certainly, the next generation of wearable health technologies will include sensors that detect physiological indicators and pathological markers that not only help clinicians and patients evaluate physiological activities, but can also help providers diagnose, treat, and monitor diseases more easily. These sensors, along with AI and the IoT, form the core of the most exciting developments, such as revolutionary biocompatible biosensors.

• • •

Biosensors can detect all kinds of information about your body's health. Basically, there are currently three different kinds making researchers and clinicians feverish with excitement: the wearable kind, which typically functions on your skin; biosensors that you swallow or are introduced into your GI tract in another way; and implantable biosensors that function inside the body, usually in direct contact with tissue.[3]

Wearable biosensors on the skin can detect heart rate, blood oxygen saturation, blood pressure, and respiratory rate. The idea here is that your wearable sensors can detect signals from your body and transmit information via digital devices to you and your clinician about changes in your condition, vital signs, or disease progression.

One simple version of how this might work in the future could be that bracelet they give you to wear in the hospital. Hospital bracelets have traditionally been printed with your name and date of birth, so care providers won't mix you up with other patients at the hospital. Now imagine that this bracelet contains biosensors that can track your vital signs, maybe even after you leave the hospital, and transmit that information to your physician. That could vastly improve post-hospital recovery, because markers such as abnormal changes in body temperature can indicate changes in your cognitive status or how a wound is healing. Wearable healthcare devices have an advantage over things like blood pressure cuffs and stethoscopes, because they provide a multi-functional platform with sensors that can detect a lot of things at once. These devices are also portable and comfortable, so people can use them in or outside their homes.

Wearable devices with biosensors may soon replace even more complex diagnostics such as electrocardiograms; even now, patients with heart issues are often sent home with a monitor they can wear for a couple of weeks to track their heart activity in real time for their providers.

Another example of wearable health technology already in use is smart contact lenses. These lenses introduce biosensors into the eye, allowing ophthalmologists to diagnose and treat eye diseases like glaucoma. In addition, biosensors are helpful in body movement testing, which is an essential part of rehabilitation medicine for people with Parkinson's or Alzheimer's disease.

For testing, monitoring, and providing treatments that can't be done through wearable sensors on the skin, researchers are developing ingestible biosensing capsules (IBCs). These are designed to travel through your gastrointestinal (GI) tract and cozy up to your organs. So far, they seem like worthy candidates for diagnostics, and maybe even for surgical or pharmaceutical therapies.

There are both "passive" and "active" IBCs. The passive devices basically flow down your GI tract with the gastric juices and sense physiological markers, like gas or pH, in endoscopy procedures, carrying tiny multi-camera systems through your gut. Some are magnetically controlled. Other, more active IBC devices have spidery legs that anchor them to intestinal walls, or corkscrew-like propellers.

Ingestible sensors are being designed to monitor lots of different health indices, from tissue appearance to biomarkers like electrolytes in a patient's GI tract, and have the potential to monitor health conditions like gut inflammation.

Finally, there are implantable biosensors, which are possible to design and manufacture now that we've created materials that are more compatible with the human body. These implantable devices have great potential in both diagnostic and treatment applications. However, there are still concerns about the body's immune responses to them, as these devices come into contact with blood and tissue. Right now these devices are mostly being tested for neuromonitoring diseases like Parkinson's and epilepsy, and for evaluating the effects of surgical electrical stimulation in treating certain neurological conditions.

The bottom line is that biocompatible biosensors, some of which are already on the market, are revolutionizing healthcare technology. At some point they're bound to replace, or at least supplement, traditional diagnostics and treatments as AI algorithms continue to make wearable health technologies increasingly stable and accurate.

One example of wearable health technology already in use is Great Lakes NeuroTechnologies' Kinesia system. With this system, patients with Parkinson's wear a sensor and have tablet-based software that collects data from it, gives out patient instructions, and transmits all data to a cloud service. Their physicians can then access the data through a portal and find out how the disease is progressing and how the patient is coping.

Another recent development is FAST (which stands for Flexible Autonomous Sensor measuring Tumors), a battery-powered wearable device developed by Stanford University researchers that can measure cancer tumors. According to an article that appeared in 2022, "the FAST sensor consists of a thin layer of gold sensors embedded in a stretchable, skin-like polymer material. The sensors detect minute changes in tumor size and shape by reacting to stretching or contraction of the patch."[4]

So far, FAST has only been used in animal studies to test cancer drugs on mice with subcutaneous tumors, but it's cheap to build (about $60 as of this writing), it's reusable, and it offers rapid real-time data. FAST is the first tool that has the potential to provide real-time analysis of tumors in vivo. This device has the potential to track tumor growth that may prove to be a lot more effective than today's diagnostic imaging or physicians measuring tumors with metal calipers in the traditional "pinch test" many doctors still rely on today.[5]

• • •

Of course, wearable health technology, just like AI, brings with it concerns about ethics and security, since much more of a person's life will be online than ever before. But it's here to stay. Our guess is that all of us will soon be wearing devices that can perform local data analysis and send that data to alert our caregivers when we need treatment. These devices will likely also share our medications and health updates with our providers through some kind of online gateway.

Our healthcare providers will more easily be able to track our health statistics using this technology, anticipating possible issues before they even arise. This could make healthcare cheaper overall because we'll get preventive interventions instead of treatments for diseases that have already manifested. And just in time, too, as the population in the United States continues to age and we experience more of a shortfall in primary care providers.

So far, the only wearable health technology I've used is a Dexcom G6 continuous glucose monitoring system that syncs with my phone and captures my sugar levels day and night. This system warns me when my sugar is too high or too low, and gives me my A1C after ninety days. I also wear an Apple Watch for my heart; this device gives me my BPM (beats per minute). I check it whenever I feel like my heart is racing. (It's always fine.)

Wearable health technology reassures me that I'm okay, which is great for keeping my illness anxiety at bay. Alternatively, if there is something wrong, I can do something about it. This kind of knowledge removes a lot of uncertainty, which is what hypos like me struggle with day to day, or even minute to minute.

Once I get *all* of the monitors on the marketplace, I'll probably have to get strip-searched by the TSA when I set off all the alarms in the airport, but it'll be totally worth it. The only thing I'll have to worry about after I start wearing every device available is becoming a lightning rod and killing myself in the midst of a thunderstorm.

Marnie's Take on Wearable Technology

One of the most important things I've learned about healthcare by working with Hal Rosenbluth is that flexibility is critical to success in the face of a rapidly changing business landscape, especially in healthcare. It's important when it comes to leadership and making decisions, especially with IT strategy.

The beauty of New Ocean Healthcare Solutions is that Hal's leadership attracts curious problem solvers and nimble thinkers. The result is that we've designed a health platform that's built for today's and tomorrow's healthcare landscape. Open APIs boast flexibility beyond imagination of the next wearable or Bluetooth-enabled medical devices, and connect seamlessly with over 375 and growing HITRUST (health information trust alliance security measures) we have taken to ensure data that's secure.

The question in my mind pertains to whether wearable health tech instigates a hypervigilance about our well-being, therefore contributing to illness anxiety. If that's the case, this could result in higher utilization of ER and healthcare services and ultimately elevate costs.

Conversely, could our heightened self-awareness lead to better preventive and proactive behaviors, as Hal suggests? If so, that may some day culminate in a healthier society, one in which we actively manage our health and drive down costs in the long run.

There's a complex balance between these possibilities in understanding the broader implications of wearables. I believe that an end-to-end digital solution is a scalable reality of our future and will help manage illness anxiety. One focus of New Ocean Health Solutions that's particularly relevant to hypochondria is anxiety management. Our digital tool is based on dialectical behavioral therapy. This is similar to cognitive behavioral therapy (CBT), which we'll discuss in Chapters 14 and 15, but uses four skills to help people accept their life condition: 1) mindfulness, 2) distress tolerance, 3) interpersonal effectiveness, and 4) emotional regulation. Our platform is designed to connect with stress-reducing wearable devices.

A lot of these devices have simple designs that can't yet address the complex conditions such as stress or anxiety which have multiple triggers and symptoms. One example of this is the measure of sweat volume or a rapid heartbeat, which don't always add up to anxiety. (Think of those early glitches in the Apple Watch going off when descending quickly on a plane.)

The New Ocean platform can take all data sources in, but it's the combination of the evidence-based medicine behind it (the journaling, the toolbox to help people meditate or manage relationships, the ability to record exercises or track symptoms) that's helping us in our AI progress. In Chapter 15, we'll share more about our view on the velocity of change, the costs of healthcare, and some future considerations.

CHAPTER FOURTEEN

Living with Uncertainty

A couple of summers ago, I experienced back pain that lasted a month or so. I had no idea why. I couldn't remember injuring myself, so I assumed it must be muscle pain. I stretched dutifully every morning, until one day my wife, Renee, found me writhing in pain on the floor and unable to stand.

Once vertical, I called my concierge physician, Dr. Killion. "I need a quick fix for my back," I said, and told him I was heading to my cattle ranch in North Dakota that weekend. "I'm going to be upright on my horse to round up hundreds of cows and calves next week, and I need to be able to bend over to castrate the bull calves during branding."

Dr. Killion listened to this request as calmly as he always listens, then said I could come in the next day for an exam.

Before the appointment, I couldn't resist a quick Google search for "When should I worry about upper back pain?" and "What organ can cause upper back pain?"

The results were as terrifying as I'd imagined. Most entries said something like this: "Organs, including kidneys and the pancreas, can cause pain that spreads to your upper back. The type of pain depends on the cause. It might feel like a continuous, dull ache or a sharp and sudden pinch."

My anxiety spiked. I'm a diabetic, which means kidney disease and conditions of the pancreas are the usual suspects when it comes to complications. Normally I see Dr. Killion alone, but this time Renee accompanied me. (I did wonder at the time whether this was out of serious concern, or whether she saw this as an opportunity to tell the doctor about my poor eating habits and ask him how it was possible for me to be losing weight when I was eating like a pig.)

Dr. Killion examined me, then escorted me to another room where I had a blood test, urinalysis, and some dip stick test. Back in the exam room, Renee spent time sharing my lifestyle habits that she felt might be contributing to my pain.

Using his best bedside manner, Dr. Killion proceeded to lecture me on daily dietary adjustments I needed to make while his assistant ordered a chest X-ray and bone density scan. Our next stop was the radiology department. On the way there, Renee said the results of the instant dip stick indicated that my white blood cells were elevated.

"Cancer?" I whispered.

"Calm down. It could also indicate a urinary tract infection or pancreatitis," she said. "If it's a UTI, you'll just take antibiotics."

"Yes, well, I've been taking amoxicillin since the dentist pulled two of my teeth last week, so I doubt that's it."

Back at home, I discovered that my back pain had mysteriously disappeared. Still, I eagerly opened the test results I'd received online and saw that one of them indicated minor degenerative thoracolumbar spine disease. Okay, not a bad result, but I was still apprehensive about what the blood test and urinalysis might uncover.

In my self-diagnosis I was leaning toward pancreatitis, since I'd convinced my endocrinologist to change my diabetes medicine a few months back. He'd shared with me that this medication might cause complications because it's related to the one that had caused me unbelievable pain in the past.

The next day, Dr. Killion called to say my test results were back. "Everything appears to be fine, Hal," he said.

"No pancreatitis?"

"No, you're good."

"But the dip stick?"

"False positive. Those things aren't all that reliable."

"So I'm good?" I asked in disbelief.

"You're good!" Dr. Killion said.

"But what about the degenerative spine disease?"

"Nothing to worry about. That's normal, given your age."

"So what's wrong with me?"

"Absolutely nothing, Hal. Relax. Go out to the ranch and rope some cows."

• • •

This year, after having gotten a very sophisticated PET-MRI to look at every part of my body and brain and hearing that doctor assure me that I'm "perfectly fine," there's absolutely nothing wrong with my organs and there's no cancer anywhere, I'm finally more confident that I'm healthy.

That scan—which, as you might recall, Dr. Killion told me I didn't need—finally removed my fear of the unknown. I am now able to say to myself, "Well, stop worrying, at least until you get your next scan."

Turns out we were both right about the scan. Dr. Killion knows more about me than a scanning device and, as he suspected, it found nothing. On the other hand, the scan gave me the emotional comfort I had been yearning for, as a sort of "second opinion technology" that found nothing. My worry went away and so has my hypochondria, for the most part—at least until my next visit to my doctor and the scan center.

So, is that the solution for hypos like me, to have a scan once a year?

The problem is that paying for a private company to do that kind of diagnostic imaging is a big, expensive reassurance, one that most people can't afford. However, once this technology scales, the price will come down dramatically. Payers will one day realize that the cost of paying for hypochondriacs to overuse the system is far greater than the cost of scans and full blood panels.

Still, what I suspect—what I *know*—will probably happen is that, after some months go by, I'll start wondering if the scan might have missed something. My swirling thoughts will go something like this: *Radiologists are just humans. They're as flawed as the rest of us! What if that guy missed something? Or what if there was something there, but it was too small at the time to be picked up by the scan?*

A scan is a temporary fix. What, then, is the solution? Is there any real cure for illness anxiety?

· · ·

As we've discussed throughout the book, illness anxiety disorder is defined by excessive worry about developing or having a potentially serious, but still undiagnosed condition. People who live under the cloud of IAD— hypochondriacs like my friend Harry and me—are often uncomfortable experiencing "normal" body sensations. We're inclined to label even the most subtle changes in our bodies as something "wrong."

Illness anxiety permeates the thoughts of those of us

who suffer from the disorder. The condition can affect our personal relationships and professional lives. Many who are less open about it than I am live with the additional burden of shame. The disorder can also cost us, and the healthcare system, a bundle of money, as we overuse doctors, emergency rooms, walk-in clinics, and laboratories. We're apt to consult multiple care providers for the same complaint and might repeat diagnostic testing even when the results are negative.

One recent study estimated that up to 20 percent of the U.S. medical budget is spent on patients who have "hypochondriacal concerns" because many patients with illness anxiety don't respond to "appropriate medical reassurance."[1] Instead, they bounce from one provider to another, or even to different ER rooms, seeking reassurances that nobody can really give us.

Or, alternatively, many people with illness anxiety avoid going to the doctor at all, because they're terrified they'll find something horribly wrong. As a friend of mine likes to say, "Doctors always find something. Better not to go." Obviously, I don't subscribe to such thinking—and recently found out that he has a medical issue that a doctor could have foreseen.

People like us need a solution.

Currently, the most popular treatments for illness anxiety are cognitive behavioral therapy (CBT) and anti-anxiety medications, typically SSRIs (selective seratonin reuptake inhibitors). One meta-analysis by researchers in the UK reported that "Hypochondriasis is a distressing condition and is associated with an increased risk of suicide." Furthermore, the analysis says that "at least one patient out of five attending medical clinics in the UK has 'some form of health-related anxiety,'" and that "the health-care costs of individuals with health anxiety . . . are 20–30% higher than the adjusted mean cost." In their final analysis, the authors of this study concluded that "both CBT and SSRIs are modestly effective for the acute treatment of hypochondriasis, but there remain key gaps in knowledge that undermine confidence in the findings."[2]

Not exactly a ringing endorsement for either treatment, but hey. We take what we can get.

Probably few people know more about using CBT to treat illness anxiety than Dr. Michael Tompkins, PhD, a psychologist who co-directs the San Francisco Bay Area Center for Cognitive Therapy. He sees CBT as a "very real and effective treatment for illness anxiety."

Tompkins views illness anxiety as a component of several anxiety disorders as well as OCD (obsessive compulsive disorder). That's what makes illness anxiety so complex to diagnose and treat. "Studies have been done that basically say about 70 to 80 percent of people with an anxiety disorder have a co-occurring anxiety or depression of some degree," he explains. "These complexities influence how well people are going to respond to any treatment."

In short, "people are complicated," Tompkins says, and it's difficult to treat someone who has lots of complications, such as health-related medical issues or trauma.

Tompkins has seen a "huge uptick" in mental health issues in the general population due to COVID, geopolitical events, financial anxiety, and a general trend toward Googling everything under the sun. (Guilty as charged.)

"People are really suffering," he says, "even with sleep. The uptick of insomnia has been huge over the last four or five years."

He points out that many people with illness anxiety are embarrassed about it. They might have friends or family members who tease them. (I certainly do.) They also become "high medical utilizers," Tompkins adds, "so they can be paying a lot of money out of pocket, even if they have insurance. If you have a lot of means, that's not a big deal. But if you don't have a lot of means, those co-pays add up."

There might be missed days of work, too, because people are spending so many hours at those doctors' appointments and getting tests and diagnostics. In extreme cases, people with illness anxiety might even be too anxious to go into the office, or so worried about their health that they just don't feel like they can focus or perform on the job.

Certainty in life is a myth. But for people with illness anxiety, it's the uncertainties that make us anxious, because we can't tolerate them enough to watch and wait. It's basically a belief that we're not capable of living with anxiety. We need to be reassured or we'll go nuts, which is why we make so many visits to doctors, and request test after test even when we're repeatedly told nothing is wrong with us. We keep overestimating that the likelihood of that ache, that pain we feel is dangerous, or even fatal. In short, illness anxiety is about being unable to tolerate uncertainty.

Certainly, in my ideal world I'd like to eliminate everything I'm anxious and uncertain about, especially my fear of cancer or some other fatal illness.

As its name suggests, the goal of CBT is to help people suffering from anxiety modify the thoughts and behaviors that cause them distress while teaching them healthier thoughts and behaviors. This therapy is based on the assumption that the emotional distress results from how people perceive their reality and interpret it.

When Tompkins treats people with CBT, he starts by sending them screening questionnaires. Then he meets with his clients to go over their answers and define the problem. CBT is different from other therapies used in psychology, he says, because "we're not so terribly interested in how the problem started, but we're very interested in treating the factors or variables that maintain it."

During CBT sessions—which typically last six to twelve weeks—the point is to "help people build up their tolerance to uncertainty," says Tompkins, "so they can organize their actions relative to probability. Then they'll be able to live their lives in more reasonable, less disruptive ways with less suffering."

During his first consultation with individuals after they've completed the questionnaires about their anxieties, Tompkins provides "a little bit of conceptualization." He describes what's happening with the person's illness anxiety and the variables he sees that keep it going. The interventions he then prescribes are meant to target those variables.

For instance, he'll say, "Let's take a particular episode when your health anxiety really kicked up. It doesn't have to be a big, big one. It doesn't have to be like you're super anxious. But tell me about a time recently which got this kicked up for you."

Then he'll discuss that situation, which is the "trigger." Maybe his client heard a Big Pharma ad, or they were at dinner with someone who mentioned that their uncle has cancer. Whatever the client says, Tompkins will then delve into it, asking, "Okay, in that moment, what were you feeling? You're anxious. Yes. All right. We're going to write that in the feeling bubble. How anxious were you on the zero to ten scale, where ten is you're freaking out, and at zero you're cool and calm? Okay, great. Between hearing your friend talk about their uncle and feeling anxious, what was going through your mind?"

The person might say, "Well, what if that ache that I had the other day is cancer?"

Tompkins will go from there, unpacking for the client the things they did when a health-related worry made them anxious, and identifying those actions as "behaviors."

Maybe they started peppering the friend with questions, because they wanted to find out if the pain they're having is like the pain the sick uncle may be experiencing. Then they went home and consulted Google.

Tompkins might then ask, "Do you go to Dr. Google a lot?"

If the person says yes, Tompkins will just nod and ask, "And then what happened?"

"Well, I did go to Dr. Google and I just kept looking at it," the client might say. "At first, I found something that helped me feel a little anxious, but I just still felt kind of uncertain. And so I just kept Googling. And then I hit something that really, really made me anxious."

What Tompkins is basically doing as he talks through these scenarios is helping patients "conceptualize the pieces." This breaks down the behaviors into the patient's responses to triggers, thoughts, feelings, and actions. This is important, he explains, because not everyone is aware of their own thought processes. "In the cognitive model, it's essential that people are aware of what they're thinking. And so that's the first step."

Once patients understand what they're thinking and the role that plays in how they're feeling, and in how that thinking impacts their actions, they can start to work on those anxious actions. Depending on what kind of illness anxiety they're experiencing, he might teach them some progressive muscle relaxation or mindfulness strategies such as focusing on breathing, and recognizing what event or circumstances triggered the anxiety.

The next step is to help them alter their thinking when those triggers cause anxiety. He does this in a very literal sense, using a whiteboard to illustrate how they can evaluate their thoughts and what their "thinking errors" might be, as well as some cognitive interventions around that. Together they then develop a plan to resist "safety behaviors" the next time an event triggers their anxiety.

For the client who was triggered by hearing about a friend's sick uncle, for instance, Tompkins would work on helping the person tolerate the anxiety of not running to Google every time they hear something like that.

He might also do some "imaginal exposures" in which they basically make a recording of triggering words and phrases, like "I have cancer." Listening to that recording multiple times can help people strengthen their belief that they can tolerate the thought of having cancer.

Or, if someone is avoiding going to the doctor because they're afraid they'll get terrible news, Tompkins might ask the person to drive to their local hospital and park outside. "We're going to have a ladder," he tells them, "and the first rung on the ladder is that you're going to go to the hospital and you're going to just sit in your car and look at the hospital."

"Oh gosh, that makes me really anxious. I don't even like to look at hospitals," the patient might say.

Tompkins will encourage the client to get more comfortable driving over to the hospital and parking outside just to look at the building. When they're comfortable with that, he'll ask them to go into the waiting room and sit there, watching sick people walk by until that doesn't make them anxious.

Eventually, through repeated exposures to emotional triggers and situations that people are avoiding, as well as teaching them calming techniques and different ways of thinking and feeling about these things, the anxiety will usually lessen to a tolerable level—often in a matter of six to twelve weeks.

The bottom line, Tompkins says, is that "exposures are engineered by the therapist and the patient to create an experience that is repeatable in a relatively short period of time. So when you treat health anxiety, or any anxiety disorder, the central, active, powerful ingredient is emotion exposure. If you're working with someone who's not doing emotion exposure, you're not getting CBT."

• • •

Will I try CBT? Probably not. I'm happy it works for other people, but I don't like people getting into my head unless I totally trust them. For instance, I'll let my wife, Renee, in my head and more recently my coauthor, Marnie, because I not only trust her, but she has a 100 percent track record of giving me medical advice that I believe turns out to be correct.

CBT is a first line of defense against anxiety, but I have yet to try it. I think initially I was concerned that my visit to a therapist might involve a discussion delving into my childhood and the unfortunate incident involving my pet snake, filled with questions about whether I enjoyed feeding him mice—almost in a stereotypical psychoanalytical Freudian fashion. However, I've come to realize that discussions can be beneficial for addressing anxiety and overall well-being. I do believe that many psychologists are genuinely compassionate and dedicated professionals who work with people to help them feel understood and empowered rather than crazy.

Over time, I've progressed from being a hopeless hypochondriac to becoming a cognitive hypochondriac, so I tend to better understand what's going on than other people might. I can deal with my illness anxiety mainly by going to my doctor, who will tell me if there is anything to worry about.

I take pride in my emotional intelligence and believe that it's important to keep an open mind and a positive attitude, and that when I am ready, I would enjoy an approach that includes engaging discussion with a psychologist about their own experiences and perspectives.

Until then I have, however, tried the second line of defense against most types of anxiety, which is pharmacological. Anti-anxiety medication seems to keep me on a more even keel, as does medical marijuana. I have also attempted other therapeutic methods and have had varying degrees of success.

For instance, we formed New Ocean Health Solutions as a health and wellness company, so we're always testing out technologies, methods, and trending activities for keeping people healthy. For example, yoga sessions, free trials for the newest health app, and having dedicated spaces for meditation are all part of the culture we espouse at New Ocean.

I did some yoga for a while, just to get limber enough so I could cross my legs when I was being interviewed on TV. It worked for that, but didn't do much for my anxiety. The problem was that it was truly awkward doing yoga in that room with all of my coworkers getting into these weird positions, some of which cause flatulence. I couldn't stop thinking about how awkward I must look.

We were also testing out some meditation apps, so one day when I was feeling especially stressed, I clomped into our office meditation room in my cowboy boots to listen to one of them. It was a great space, outfitted with a massage chair and some kind of high-end salt lamp. I thought for sure I'd at least be able to take a nap if I wore those headphones and listened to the app for a while.

No such luck. About fifteen minutes into it, I clomped back out of the room and shook my head at Marnie and our clinical staff, who reside opposite "the room."

"I can't do this," I said.

"What's the matter, Hal? Why not?" she asked.

"This guy's voice is driving me crazy," I said. "He's whispering like a pedophile trying to lure me into a windowless van."

Many people find meditation and guided imagery apps very helpful, but they weren't exactly the breakthrough solution for me. Yet being dedicated to a continuous exploration to discover just the right solution has been invaluable to me during the process of writing this book. The one thing that consistently works to lower my anxiety is going out to the ranch. When I really started to think about why that might be, I came up with various answers, like not being around other hypochondriacs, not being triggered by seeing hospitals and pharmacies everywhere, not watching the same kinds of TV programs with Big Pharma ads, and being too physically engaged to worry much about whether I have cancer. Finally, it dawned on me that maybe it's just being outside and physically active so much of the time that makes me feel much less anxious.

There's a lot of research to support this idea. Researchers have known for a long time that exercise reduces stress at every level, and that being outdoors helps just about everyone feel better. Now there's a new practice called "forest therapy" that's growing in popularity worldwide. Forest therapy is inspired by the Japanese practice of "forest bathing," or "Shinrin-yoku."

In one study, the authors found that forest bathing had positive physiological effects on participants, such as lowering blood pressure, improving autonomic and immune functions, alleviating depression, and boosting overall mental health. These same authors report that, in the UK, "depression treatment guidelines identify that exposure to the outdoors and a forest environment promotes resilience."[3] An unrelated study, also in the UK, found that among almost twenty thousand people surveyed, spending at least two hours a week in nature improved self-reported health.[4]

Forest therapy simply takes this a step further, offering

people a "guided outdoor healing practice."[5] Trained guides set a deliberately slow pace as they invite people to be fully present in their bodies and use all their senses in the natural world. In test subjects, levels of cortisol—a stress hormone that plays a role in everything from heart disease to headaches—were lowered after walking in a forest, which didn't happen when people walked in a laboratory setting.

So maybe I'm not completely crazy, and spending time out on my ranch really is, for me, the best therapy of all.

CHAPTER FIFTEEN

Solutions to Improve Our Country's Health

At this writing, the main problem our healthcare system faces nationally is a way to provide access to quality care in an equitable manner to all populations. That means providing care in a way that is both more immediate and seamlessly connected. The shortage of providers looms large as an issue, too. People living with illness anxiety disorder both highlight and exacerbate the issues of inequitable, costly healthcare, as I have found in navigating the healthcare system and shared with you in this book.

So what's the answer? How can we deliver more accessible, affordable, top-quality healthcare to all, while addressing the additional burden people with hypochondria place on our national system?

Marnie's Take

Here's the imprint left on me through the process of writing this book: Hal's journey through the healthcare system as a hypochondriac has been comprised of multiple stops along the way. Even without the research we've done, it's clear that the sheer volume of Hal's medical claims and tests highlight the impact that illness anxiety disorder can have not only on individuals suffering from hypochondria, but also on the traditional delivery of care in our healthcare system.

The system we currently have in place can't fix Hal's anxiety. He used his considerable resources to create his own brilliantly designed individual healthcare system, one that is based on providing him with answers to his healthcare questions and the highest-quality care whenever he has a health concern.

Like all of us, Hal wants immediate care when he has a health problem, as well as treatments that provide instant relief. The difference between him as a hypochondriac and those of us who don't suffer from illness anxiety is that he can't live with unknown variables. That's clear from his constant Googling, his willingness to take multiple drugs for multiple conditions, and his decisions to pay for both a full-body scan and a concierge doctor to put his mind at ease.

In some ways, Hal's healthcare decisions reflect his business and leadership style, which is based on curiosity; the art of the possible; and fulfilling unknown, unmet needs through innovation. As it happens, that combination of his insatiable curiosity and his need for instant gratification also reveal the technological blueprint that many industries have embraced to revolutionize healthcare services and provide convenience to their consumers. This includes our company, New Ocean Health Solutions.

Hal's use of technology on the ranch is another great example of how technology can be used as a springboard for healthcare solutions—especially solutions that can mitigate the burden of hypochondria on the system. Every spring and summer, he heads out to the ranch to tend to his cattle, horses, and fields. As far away as that seems, he's never out of reach. He takes morning meetings with executives while he's on his tractor via Microsoft Teams app, using the iPad he has assembled on the front control. He can also respond to emails or calls this way.

Hal's usual water-cooler banter at the office is replaced with group texts when he's in North Dakota. He often leads with an update on the latest horse breaking, calf roping, or weather report. Droughts are big news because it means Hal and his partners have to leave Linton to find other hydrated places to hay. He also reports on other calamities of ranch life, like his last encounter with a wasp nest and his description of a full-throttle speed run for his EpiPen, which was miles from where he was on his horse. Sometimes there are graphic pictures, too, of a broken, bloody, this-or-that animal or human part, usually accompanied by the caption "today" to keep the connection warm.

Mobile technology has figured importantly into the

success of our business, and Hal has the best of all possible worlds. With one finger, he can virtually transport himself from the barn to the boardroom with a yard-long list of questions and directives for my colleagues and me.

This concept of being constantly connected is essential to the future of better healthcare. Technology is helping us develop solutions that can mitigate the underlying costs of hypochondria and Big Pharma's pill paradigm. Our society needs better access and connectedness to cost-efficient, quality healthcare. Technology can help us develop solutions that expand our finite resources of time, people, money, and energy instead of draining them. Every other industry has revolutionized its services thanks to digital technology; at New Ocean, we intend to be part of the revolutionary movement now dragging healthcare into the next century and beyond.

An end-to-end care solution that solves our healthcare crises can seem like the Holy Grail when we're faced with solving the complex dilemmas of the great imbalances in healthcare utilization. On the one hand, we have underutilization of healthcare by those who truly need it. Barriers to care include social determinants of health, such as access to transportation, nutritious food and medicine, health care coverage, education and health literacy and financial stability. As we've discussed in this book, these barriers too often lead people to seek care in the high-cost setting of the emergency room, where treating chronic conditions can be more challenging and less effective.

On the other hand, we have overutilization of the system by people with illness anxiety, like Hal. Hypochondriacs can be on both sides of this seesaw since, as we've already described, some people with illness anxiety are crippled by their fear of serious illness, and therefore avoid health tests and physicians' visits. This can lead to more expensive care in the long run.

These healthcare highflyers are driven by their hypochondria into a continuous search for immediate reassurances. Too often, they too eat up ER time and physicians' appointments, in their case because they can't live with the anxiety of their uncertainty. This fruitless search for answers and cures to imagined illnesses not only drives up costs for them and for healthcare insurers, but also diverts resources away from those who genuinely need care. Most patient consumers fall somewhere in between those two categories of those who want faster service and instant gratification and those who don't even know they require medical attention or lack the resources to get it. Navigating toward a greater balance and efficiency in our nation's healthcare system will require a multifaceted approach. This should include several areas:

Preventive Care and Health Literacy—Raising awareness about important screenings, especially for those with chronic conditions or risk factors (these could be environmental, behavioral, or medically historical in nature). An added perk: Empowering people with information can help ease illness anxiety and circumvent more unnecessary medical testing, ER time, and clinic visits.

Equitable Access—Breaking down barriers like geography, cultural differences, and affordability can shorten the bridge to healthcare. The solution needed to achieve this lies in large part in making better use of telehealth and remote patient monitoring, since those provide more accessible, affordable care by reducing the frequency of in-person visits. For people with illness anxiety, telehealth can also remove the stigma of seeking care so often.

Managing Anxiety—We must continue working on de-stigmatizing mental health and do much more to provide support for psychological services to those suffering from depression and anxiety in any form, including illness anxiety. This will result in a better allocation of resources, helping us manage healthcare costs more effectively and preserve the integrity of services.

Encouraging Holistic Care Over Pharmaceuticals—
Pharmaceutical interventions have brought infinite benefits
to healthcare. However, the paradigm of "the quick fix" isn't
a sustainable solution. In fact, we have seen an unhealthy
overmedicalization of America. Our dependency on pills
carries the risks of side effects. More important, if people
are reaching for pills first, it leaves them less motivated to
explore holistic healthy lifestyle changes that can address
many chronic conditions. Providers need to be encouraged
to examine the root causes of health problems such as poor
diet, sedentary lifestyles, and chronic stress. They should be
trained to inform their patients about alternative options and
encourage them to try those treatments first. As I described
in Chapter 3, going to physical therapy was the best decision
I ever made when I hurt my shoulder, because it built my
strength from the inside out. In fact, PT brought back my
confidence and inspired me to resume my interest in fitness
training, which had the happy side effects of reducing my
stress levels and increasing my productivity. Isn't this what
we all want?

• • •

One thing we haven't discussed to any great extent in the
book is the future of AI (artificial intelligence) and its ability
to transform the future of healthcare. AI has the potential to

help address both the additional burden of cost put on the healthcare system by hypochondriacs and the efficiency of our healthcare system in general.

We have already witnessed what AI can do in other arenas, thanks to "The crazy ones. The misfits. The rebels. The troublemakers. The round pegs in the square holes. The ones who see things differently. They're not fond of rules. And they have no respect for the status quo. You can quote them, disagree with them, glorify or vilify them. About the only thing you can't do is ignore them. Because they change things. They push the human race forward."[1] These are the words of Steve Jobs who, in 1997, made everyone "think different" and gave a nod to every great innovator who came before him.

There is a lot of public mistrust around the use of AI. This is ironic, because we've already been using it for years. How do people think Google Maps works? AI has also transformed the way we shop, allowing Amazon and other e-commerce companies to provide fast deliveries and easy returns.

While of course there are still barriers to using technology—like having a smartphone, Wi-Fi service, and a credit card—most people are using AI technology every day to discover and deliver the services they need. Data analytics and AI-based algorithms currently serve up personal recommendations for which books, movies, and products you might like. We no longer have to get into our cars or carry bags of groceries from the garage, since online services like DoorDash and Uber Eats have that covered. Nor do we stand in line for concert or theater tickets anymore, because they're delivered straight to our in-boxes when we buy the tickets online.

Now companies are taking a greater leap into tech to bridge the gaps of affordable, accessible, high-quality healthcare. By the time this book is published, New Ocean Health Solutions, along with many other tech companies operating in the healthcare arena, will probably have come up with new solutions for care. Leveraging the immense potential of AI technologies to deliver better, more easily accessed healthcare will improve our health outcomes and lower the overall burden on the ecosystem. Here are some of the AI advances that have already made guest appearances in healthcare:

- **Telehealth Visits**—AI-powered telehealth platforms enable patients to consult with care providers, virtually negating the need for in-person visits in many instances. In fact, in many ways, providers spend more quality time on-screen than they do with patients on the exam table.

- **Remote Monitoring**—Remote patient monitoring devices provide real-time health data to healthcare providers, allowing for proactive interventions.

- **Diagnoses and Treatments**—AI algorithms assist radiologists by analyzing medical images such as X-rays and MRIs. AI can also provide recommendations for appropriate treatment options based on patient data and evidenced-based medicine.

- **Personalized Medicine**—Intelligent claims data analysis can sort data and medical histories to tailor treatment plans, predict risks, trigger messages to close gaps in care, and identify the most effective medications based on patient history. This is key in reducing or avoiding side effects and increasing medication adherence.

- **Predictive Analytics**—By analyzing vast amounts of healthcare data, AI research tools can better manage population health by predicting risks and disease patterns. AI can also improve patient outcomes by mitigating risk of major outbreaks.

- **Wearable health tech**—Apple Watches and other medical-grade devices monitor vital signs like heart rate and blood pressure, and can alert individuals and healthcare providers to potential health issues. This can advance early detection, intervention, and treatment.

- **Administration**—Chatbots relieve humans of administrative tasks like appointment scheduling, billing, and insurance claims processing. This reallocates funds to support other job functions.

- **Research**—AI can analyze models, drug effectiveness, and medication interactions, potentially reducing the time and cost of developing new treatments.

- **Coaching**—AI-powered chatbots provide patients with information about their conditions, medications, and treatment plans, helping patients better engage with and manage their own health.

At New Ocean Health Solutions, our current platform and the AI work we are doing will exponentially enhance the patient experience in ways that will soon be the standard of care. Adopting AI in healthcare is exciting, but it comes with quite a few challenges. Most of these center around data security and privacy, risk compliance, and the necessary training doctors and staff will need to use some of these tools.

Overall, however, we believe that integrating AI will allow doctors to give higher quality care; provide a greater bandwidth for providers, especially in the mental health space, so they can take on more cases; offer more efficient and accurate diagnoses; provide better monitoring; and inspire a shift toward even more proactive, preventive healthcare.

In many ways, Hal's hypochondria inspires the kind of continuous health monitoring that, instead of being the focal point, will be happening in the background for all patients. With an end-to end, AI-assisted platform, there is a greater chance of balancing out utilization and expanding care to a scalable, more cost-efficient way to care for the underserved in both urban and rural communities.

This platform will also provide infinite reassurances for hypochondriacs, which will bring down the burden of cost they put on our healthcare system. People with illness anxiety who are constantly monitored will no doubt find comfort, as Hal did, in having their uncertainties answered. At any given moment, for instance, they will know whether their blood pressure is truly skyrocketing or only feels that way. Their digital coach can meanwhile remind them to take deep breaths, take a walk, and get some sleep, then call their doctors in the morning if things don't improve.

• • •

The End. Or Is It?

Throughout this book I've shared how I've progressed from being a hypochondriac to becoming a cognitive hypochondriac. I have weaned myself off illness anxiety disorder to the point at which I believe it no longer takes up much rent in the apartment house I call my mind.

Toward the end of this journey, I was becoming exhausted from hearing everyone say, "There's nothing wrong with you." In response, I started keeping things to myself, at least where my family was concerned. This avoided confrontations, but required me to constantly evict medical concerns from my mind and get on with life.

Was this the right thing to do? I have no idea, but at least I didn't have to defend my concerns while losing the battle to raised eyebrows and a dismissal of my symptoms.

And then it happened. My most recent medical issue turned out to be real, not imaginary, yet I decided to deal with it myself rather than share it with my family.

That medical saga began on a day when I was riding out in the hills, looking for a sick calf. The day before, I'd seen the calf lying in the tall prairie grass halfway up a steep hill, half a mile from my ranch house, while I was out on my horse and checking on the rest of the herd. The herd was miles away and I hadn't seen the calf's mother with her for a few days. Obviously, something was wrong. The calf needed to be found or it would soon die.

I decided to take my John Deere Gator to look for the calf in case I needed to use it to carry the animal back to the barn. I headed down to the pasture while my neighbor Dave took a four-wheeler and searched other parts of the land for the calf. When I reached a creek, I had to jump off the Gator because it wouldn't make it across. I headed up the hill on foot toward the place where I'd last seen the calf in the grass.

After a few minutes of walking up the hill, I found myself short of breath. This was something abnormal for me to experience while here on my ranch. Three years earlier, during a catheter examination, my cardiologist had uncovered some blockage in one of my arteries; at that time, he had suggested we take the conservative approach and go the medication route for a while before deciding on a stent.

I climbed back onto my Gator and returned to the ranch house. When I got to an area with cell service, I called the cardiology department and left a message for my doctor to give me a shout. When my cardiologist called back, I discussed the situation, and was nicely reminded that I had never followed up with him. "It's been three years since that catheter exam, Hal," he said. "Why don't you come see me in Philadelphia when you get back from the ranch?"

I did that, and the results from my visit indicated that I needed a nuclear stress test and an echocardiogram as soon as possible. The following week I was injected with isotopes, spun around in some contraption that was apparently taking pictures, and then hooked up to an ECG machine before I jumped on a treadmill.

As the technicians increased the speed and elevation of

the treadmill, I felt like I was once again looking for my lost calf. A few feet away, a doctor and an assisting Fellow whispered to each other while pointing to the ECG paper scrolling in front of them, pointing stuff out to each other. Not exactly a comforting feeling, but I knew they wouldn't share anything with me; they would send the results to my cardiologist, who would call me later in the day.

Once that stress test was over, I was injected with additional isotopes and sent back for the after-pictures of my heart. After ten minutes of turning in circles for the second set of pictures, I went off for an echocardiogram. A very nice technician hooked me up again with as many wires as our local electrical company used to restore power after the last storm hit the area. Thirty minutes later, I was wiping off more gel from my body than I had used on my hair in a month during my younger years.

The call from my cardiologist came later that day, while I was eating dinner with my family. Everyone stopped eating as I went to another room to get the verdict. Of course, my family is blessed with bionic ears, so by the time I returned to the table there was little to explain. The cardiologist reported that I needed a catheterization and said he'd most likely put a stent in this time. He also planned to perform an expedition around the rest of my heart and arteries that would make the Lindblad *Explorer* jealous as he checked for any other heart disease that might present itself.

"You'll get a call tomorrow from my nurse to set up the appointment," he said.

Around midday, the nurse called to explain. the procedure and told me what not to do or take a day in advance. She reminded me that I'd have the second fasting blood test in a week and would need to fast again the night before the procedure. "You'll be given a drug that will make you woozy, but you'll still be awake during the procedure," she added.

I protested in vain that I wanted the anesthetic drug propofol, which was the only reason I was excited to go in the first place. "No," the nurse said, "because we're going to use a type of twilight anesthesia. You'll be sedated but conscious. That's because, depending on the extent of what they have to do, they might want to wake you up and discuss next steps. By the way, you might be admitted overnight."

So, no propofol and no outpatient procedure. Not a good start to the medical equivalent of Christopher Columbus's search for the New World.

Not wanting to be awakened, I suggested that they not wake me up, but rather do what they needed to do and tell me later. Turns out that I had a 99 percent blockage in my right artery. One percent more, and it would have required bypass surgery. As it turned out, the calf I was looking for saved my life.

I've now finished proofreading this book while waiting

to be released from the hospital after the catheterization procedure and insertion of a stent. I ended up being admitted to the hospital overnight for observation. I figured, how bad could that be? I'd watch the Phillies on TV, be fed without calling Door Dash, and get a good night's sleep.

Turns out, I was awakened every hour or two. I had my blood taken six times, an EKG four times, my glucose level checked four times, my blood pressure taken eight times. Oh, and I had to piss in a jar, since I was strapped to the bed by more wires than can be found in our data room back at headquarters.

The good news is that, for the moment, I have no worries, as the procedure was a success and my artery was repaired.

So, what's next? What medical issue might befall me, or not?

Who knows? Certainly not me. Welcome to my world, the world of uncertainty, which a hypochondriac like me inhabits and has to learn to live with despite our anxiety.

Oh, and by the way, the calf died.

(Sad, but searching for it likely is what saved my life.)

Marnie's Take: Embracing The Truth of Hypochondria's Fact and Fiction

Like so many of Hal's friends and family, I grew weary of the false alarms, the short-of-breath moments that always turned out to be just fine. I'm sure that I contributed to Hal feeling like the boy who cried wolf too many times in that famous fairy tale.

Now, as we're putting the finishing touches on this book, I am thinking about the time I've spent with Hal and the role I've played in documenting his illness anxiety and telling his story as he navigates the healthcare system. I feel that in addition to writing and doing research and maintaining my role at the company as chief marketing and strategy officer, I've also become Hal's personal chief medical officer in charge of his hypochondria.

I feel terrible that as Hal recently made his way through the catheterization procedure to receive a stent, I hadn't believed him. After all, even a broken clock is right twice a day. I really felt guilty for having thought he was overdramatizing the doctor's order for an exploratory cath.

However, this remorse was somewhat quelled whenever I envisioned him calling me to say, in that complaining voice, "See, I told you I was sick!"

In the end, though, what really struck me about this latest event was that Hal suddenly seemed less anxious, and he was managing his hypochondria on his own.

A week after receiving the stent, Hal was scheduled to be the keynote speaker at a wellness summit in Philadelphia. His topic was "Love Them or Lose Them: How Much Are Your Employees Worth? Talent Retention, Resiliency, and the Hidden Impact of Mental Health."

In the past, depending on Hal's role and the length of his speech, I would have worked with him to prepare notes and slides. This time, though, he said, "I've got this. You don't need to prepare anything for this speech."

I was relieved, because honestly, Hal is not a man who sticks to a script. His remarks usually jump the guardrails regardless of how high I set them. Still, the day before his address, we talked about the speech, and I asked if he planned to share anything about his own mental health, particularly his hypochondria, since he has included that topic in past speeches.

"Of course," Hal said.

But, to my surprise, when he spoke this time, Hal didn't even mention hypochondria. After the speech, we sat in the greenroom across the main hall where everyone was still assembled, and I asked him why.

He shrugged. "I don't need to talk about it."

"At all? With anyone?" I asked.

"No. It doesn't do any good," he said.

"Is that because you feel like 'the boy who cried wolf'?" I asked. "Is it because we've stopped paying attention? Because I, for one, really feel awful about brushing off your complaints, especially when we were out at the ranch with Judd. Now I understand that you were really short of breath when doing anything strenuous, and the video production that week had you rushing around."

"No," Hal said. "It wasn't about what happened at the ranch. I think I just got tired of everyone rolling their eyes at me. Plus, my constant complaining proved to be a very unproductive use of time, so I started doing something about it."

So what did Hal do, to relieve his anxiety and tame his hypochondria?

For one thing, as he wrote this book, Hal began to examine his anxiety and recognized that many of his worries about his health were based on unfounded fears of the unknown that could be addressed through diagnostic tests like the full body scan. Science was something he could count on. As one of Hal's support team members while he wrote this book, I learned to listen to him express emotions, but I challenged his negative thoughts and pushed him to get real assurances from tests rather than wallow in fear about symptoms real or imagined.

And, even though Hal has repeatedly said he would never try cognitive behavioral therapy (CBT), in writing this book he was also leaning into the core principles of CBT. For instance, he learned that his illness anxiety was largely based on unhelpful ways of thinking and behavior patterns. His symptoms were almost always triggered by a thought or a question, that big, scary "What if?"

That led him to repeatedly chase relief from his uncertainty through doctors, online symptom checkers, and emergency appointments. Ultimately, Hal discovered that changing his thoughts, and perhaps changing his behaviors, could make him less of a hypochondriac.

Essentially, Hal was practicing many of the strategies used in CBT therapy, such as:

Journaling—Hal began to write a lot about his anxiety in the process of writing this book, recording his thoughts and noticing when his anxiety was triggered and where he was when it happened. Becoming familiar with his own anxiety was his first step in managing it. More than reflecting—which is just more thinking—writing about his anxiety was key to building his awareness and becoming more mindful about recognizing triggers. Seeing it in black and white after the anxiety passed is how Hal and others with illness anxiety begin to break the cycle.

Challenging Core Beliefs—In the past, Hal would try to ignore the anxiety, hurling it away from himself. However, this caused it to boomerang back with equal force. "It's happening again," he'd say. Instead of examining the feeling, he focused on the thought (however cognitively flawed it was). As I presented Hal with new research and he read more about illness anxiety research, as well as tools and strategies for managing it, he started to see how his thoughts were connected to his behaviors, and yes, to the very symptoms he felt. This work helped him transition from being a hypochondriac to being a cognizant hypochondriac.

Worry Period Exercises—In CBT, "worry period" exercises are all about creating a specific time to worry. Hal began to really rely on Harry and Stan for this worry period. More important, he found himself becoming a voice of reason during their balls-to-the-walls, panic-stricken Boys Nights. Hal began sharing what he was learning about his own illness anxiety to help Harry and Stan tackle their own bouts of hypochondria. At the outset of work on this book, Hal said he wished he could attend a Hypochondriacs Anonymous group, so he could stand up and say, "Hello, I'm

Hal and I'm a hypochondriac." In effect, Hal has assembled his own group therapy sessions with Harry and Stan.

Although these principles worked for Hal, some of the widely practiced CBT tools, including meditation, did not. Having to sit still tends to make him dwell more on his worries. However, he has found his own happy place of relaxation on the ranch, where being in nature and connecting to the animals he cares for puts him in a more mindful state. In fact, by recognizing the difference between what he typically feels at the ranch and how he felt when he was short of breath as he searched for that sick calf, Hal saved his own life.

As a society, we have become increasingly accepting of mental illness. We now talk about it more openly. This shift is thanks in part to books like this one that raise the public's awareness of mental health issues.

I hope that one day, everyone will have greater access to providers who can competently diagnose patients with illness anxiety and offer holistic approaches to treating it, such as CBT, forest bathing, and meditation. Or, as a last resort, I hope our providers can offer medications that have been fully researched and proven to truly target this particular disorder. We can also work toward having healthcare systems create a medical billing code for illness anxiety visits to the ER, thereby providing researchers with more data.

Until then, our hope is that reading this book has allowed you to see the healthcare system from the perspective of someone battling illness anxiety, so that you can manage your own mental health issues more effectively or support anyone with hypochondria who is in need of help.

NOTES

Introduction

1. Peter J. Peterson Foundation, "Why Are Americans Paying More for Healthcare?" January 30, 2023, https://www.pgpf. org/blog/2023/01/why-are-americans-paying-more-for-healthcare.
2. All quotes in this paragraph are from Peterson Foundation, "Why Are Americans Paying."
3. David Kendall and Ladan Ahmadi, "Millions of Americans Face High Health Costs Year after Year," *Third Way*, December 19, 2022, https://www.thirdway.org/memo/millions-of-americans-face-high-health-costs-year-after-year.
4. United States Bureau of the Census, https://www.census.gov/quickfacts/fact/table/US/PST045222#PST045222.
5. Roberta Satow, "Hypochondria: The Need to Be Believed," *Psychology Today*, March 17, 2017, https://www.psychologytoday.com/us/blog/life-after-50/201703/hypochondria.
6. The Commonwealth Fund, "U.S. Health Care from a Global Perspective, 2022: Accelerating Spending, Worsening Outcomes," January 31, 2003, www.commonwealthfund.org/publications/issue-briefs/2023/jan/us-health-care-global-perspective-2022.
7. Peter J. Peterson Foundation, "How Does the U.S. Healthcare System Compare to Other Countries?" July 12, 2023, https://www.pgpf.org/blog/2023/07/how-does-the-us-healthcare-system-compare-to-other-countries.

Chapter One
The More I Watched, the Sicker I Got

(no notes)

Chapter Two
The Making of a Hypochondriac

1. JS Bamrah, Freya Dow, Roschelle Ramkisson, and Subodh Dave, "A Hitchhiker's Guide to Anxiety Disorders," *The Physician*, Vol. 8, no. 1 (May 2023), https://physicianjnl.net/index.php/phy/article/view/160.

2. Ahmad Syaukat, "Hypochondriasis: A Literature Review," *Scientia Psychiatrica*, Vol. 3, no. 1 (2022), https://scientiapsychiatrica.com/index.php/SciPsy/article/view/85/184.

3. Amy S. Chappell, "Toward a Lifestyle Medicine Approach to Illness Anxiety Disorder (Formerly Hypochondriasis)," *Am J Lifestyle Med*, Vol. 12, no. 5 *(*April 2018*)*, https://www.ncbi.nlm.nih.gov/pmc/articles/PMC6146366/.

4. Syaukat, "Hypochondriasis."

5. Syaukat.

6. Psychology Today, "The Biology of Anxiety," *Psychology Today*, June 1, 2023, https://www.psychologytoday.com/intl/basics/anxiety/the-biology-anxiety.

7. Psychology Today.

8. Arthur J. Barsky, E. John Orav, and David W. Bates, "Somatization Increases Medical Utilization and Costs Independent of Psychiatric and Medical Comorbidity," *Journal of the American Medical Association*, Vol. 62, no. 8 (August 2005),

https://jamanetwork.com/journals/jamapsychiatry/fullarti-cle/208854.

9. Barsky.

10. Dan Mangan, "Medical Bills Are the Biggest Cause of U.S. Bankruptcies," CNBC, June 13, 2023, https://www.cnbc.com/id/100840148.

Chapter Three
Is Big Pharma Advertising Good for You?

1. Tom Nichols, "Pharmaceutical Ads Give Me Hives," *The Atlantic*, April 28, 2022, https://newsletters.theatlantic.com/peacefield/61f4c3849d9e380022bdaeb9/big-pharma-tv-drug-ads-legal/.

2. Teresa Carr, "Too Many Meds? America's Love Affair with Prescription Medication," *Consumer Reports*, August 3, 2017, https://www.consumerreports.org/prescription-drugs/too-many-meds-americas-love-affair-with-prescription-medication/.

3. John LaMatinna, "Pharma TV Ads and R&D Funding," *Forbes*, March 30, 2022, https://www.forbes.com/sites/johnlamattina/2022/03/30/pharma-tv-ads-and-rd-funding.

4. Andrew Gallant, "A Growing Number of Americans Report Taking Prescription Medications Daily," *CivicScience*, January 11, 2023, https://civicscience.com/a-growing-number-of-americans-report-taking-prescription-medications-daily.

5. Natasha Parekh and William H. Shrank, "Dangers and Opportunities of Direct-to-Consumer Advertising," *Journal of General Internal Medicine,* Vol. 33, no. 5 (May 2018), https://

www.ncbi.nlm.nih.gov/pmc/articles/PMC5910355/.

6. Fierce Pharma, "Crossing the Threshold: More than Half of Physicians Restrict Access to Sales Reps," September 3, 2015, https://www.fiercepharma.com/marketing/crossing-threshold-more-than-half-of-physicians-restrict-access-to-sales-reps.

7. Robert Schmerling, "Harvard Health Ad Watch: How Direct-to-Consumer Ads Hook Us," *Harvard Health Publishing*, March 3, 2022, https://www.health.harvard.edu/blog/harvard-health-ad-watch-what-you-should-know-about-direct-to-consumer-ads-2019092017848.

8. C. Lee Ventola, "Direct-to-Consumer Pharmaceutical Advertising: Therapeutic or Toxic?" originally published in *PT*, Vol. 36, no. 10 (October 2011), accessed at https://www.ncbi.nlm.nih.gov/pmc/articles/PMC3278148/

9. Ventola.

10. Michael J. DiStefano, Jenny M. Markell, Caroline C. Doherty, et al., "Association Between Drug Characteristics and Manufacturer Spending on Direct-to-Consumer Advertising," *Journal of the American Medical Association*, Vol. 3, no. 8 (August 2022), https://jamanetwork.com/journals/jama/fullarticle/2801060.

11. Carr, "Too Many Meds?"

Chapter Four
If You're Not Depressed, You Should Be

1. Alison Gilchrist, "10 Most-Advertised Brand-Name Drugs," *Pharmacy Times*, August 27, 2015, https://www.pharmacy-times.com/view/10-most-advertised-brand-name-drugs.

2. Sara G. Miller, "1 in 6 Americans Takes a Psychiatric Drug," *Scientific American*, December 13, 2016, https://www.scientificamerican.com/article/1-in-6-americans-takes-a-psychiatric-drug/.

3. "America's State of Mind Report," *Express Scripts*, April 16, 2020, https://www.express-scripts.com/corporate/americas-state-of-mind-report

4. Donald Cherry, Michael Albert, and Linda F. McCaig, "Mental Health–Related Physician Office Visits by Adults Aged 18 and Over: United States, 2012–2014," NCHS Data Brief, June 2018, https://www.cdc.gov/nchs/products/databriefs/db311.htm.

5. Amir Garakani, James W. Murrough, Rafael C. Freire, et al., "Pharmacotherapy of Anxiety Disorders: Current and Emerging Treatment Options," *Front Psychiatry* (December 2020), https://www.ncbi.nlm.nih.gov/pmc/articles/PMC7786299/.

6. Nisha Kurani, Dustin Cotliar, and Cynthia Cox, "How Do Prescription Drug Costs in the United States Compare to Other Countries?" *Peterson KFF Health System Tracker*, February 8, 2022, https://www.healthsystemtracker.org/chart-collection/how-do-prescription-drug-costs-in-the-united-states-compare-to-other-countries.

Chapter Five
If It's Not an Illness, It's a Side Effect!

1. Justin Greiwe, Richard Honsinger, Christopher Hvisdas, et al. "Boxed Warnings and Off-Label Use of Allergy Medications: Risks, Benefits, and Shared Decision Making," *The Journal of Allergy and Clinical Immunology: In Practice*, Vol. 10, no. 12 (December 2022), https://www.sciencedirect.com/science/article/abs/pii/S2213219822008716.

2. Kathryn Anderson, "Is Hypochondria on the Rise in the United States?" CertaPet, April 21, 2023, https://www.certapet.com/is-hypochondria-on-the-rise/.

3. Anderson.

Chapter Six
Pharmaceutical Price Wars and the
PBMs Behind the Curtain

1. All quotes in this paragraph are from the American Medical Association, "Trends in Healthcare Spending," March 20, 2023, https://www.ama-assn.org/about/research/trends-health-care-spending.

Chapter Seven
The Boys Club and Cyberchondria

1. Alex Guarino, "Study Finds 89 Percent of US Citizens Turn to Google Before Their Doctor," WECT News, June 24, 2019, https://www.wect.com/2019/06/24/study-finds-us-citizens-turn-google-before-their-doctor.

2. "Digital Hypochondria By the Numbers," NetQuote, https://www.netquote.com/health-insurance/digital-hypochondria-by-the-numbers.

3. Amber Loos, "Cyberchondria: Too Much Information for the Health Anxious Patient?" *Journal of Consumer Health on the Internet*, November 22, 2013, https://www.tandfonline.com/doi/full/10.1080/15398285.2013.833452.

4. Matteo Vismara, Alberto Varinelli, Luca Pellegrini, et al., "New Challenges in Facing Cyberchondria During the Coronavirus Disease Pandemic," *Current Opinion in Behavioral Sciences*, Vol. 46, no. 10156 (August 2022), https://www.ncbi.nlm.nih.gov/pmc/articles/PMC9098916.

5. Jill M. Newby and Eoin McElroy, "The Impact of Internet-Delivered Cognitive Behavioural Therapy for Health Anxiety on Cyberchondria," *Journal of Anxiety Disorders*, Vol. 69, no. 102150 (January 2020), https://www.sciencedirect.com/science/article/abs/pii/S088761851930218X.

Chapter Eight
What COVID Taught Us about Healthcare

1. Alice Burns, "Long COVID: What Do the Latest Data Show?" KFF, January 26, 2023, https://www.kff.org/policy-watch/long-COVID-what-do-latest-data-show.

2. Ed Yong, "What COVID Hospitalization Numbers Are Missing," *The Atlantic*, May 18, 2022, https://www.theatlantic.com/health/archive/2022/05/hospitalization-covid-healthcare-burnout/629892/.

3. ANA COVID-19 Impact Survey: The Second Year, January

2022, https://www.nursingworld.org/practice-policy/work-environment/health-safety/disaster-preparedness/coronavirus/what-you-need-to-know/COVID-19-impact-assessment-survey---the-second-year/.

4. Kathryn Anderson, "Is Hypochondria on the Rise in the United States?" CertaPet, April 21, 2023, https://www.certapet.com/is-hypochondria-on-the-rise/.

5. Jonathan H. Cantor, Ryan K. McBain, Pen-Che Ho, et al., "Telehealth and In-Person Mental Health Service Utilization and Spending, 2019 to 2022," JAMA Health Forum 2023, 4(8):e232645, doi:10.1001/jamahealthforum.2023.2645.

6. Cantor.

7. World Health Organization, "COVID-19 Pandemic Triggers 25% Increase in Prevalence of Anxiety and Depression Worldwide," March 2, 2022, https://www.who.int/news/item/02-03-2022-covid-19-pandemic-triggers-25-increase-in-prevalence-of-anxiety-and-depression-worldwide.

8. OCD Center of Los Angeles, "Hypochondria (Health Anxiety)—Symptoms and Treatment," https://ocdla.com/hypochondriasis.

9. William Sage, "What the Pandemic Taught Us: The Health Care System We Have Is Not the System We Hoped We Had," *Ohio State Law Journal*, December 2021, https://moritzlaw.osu.edu/sites/default/files/2022-02/21.%20Sage_v82-5_857-68.pdf.

10. Both quotes in this paragraph are from Sage, "What the Pandemic Taught Us."

Chapter Nine
Why the ER Is the Big Box Retail Store of Healthcare

1. Centers for Disease Control and Prevention, National Center for Health Statistics, https://www.cdc.gov/nchs/fastats/emergency-department.htm.

2. Dana R. Sax, E. Margaret Warton, Dustin G. Mark, et al., "Evaluation of the Emergency Severity Index in US Emergency Departments for the Rate of Mistriage," *JAMA Network Open*, Vol. 6, no. 3 (March 2023), https://jamanetwork.com/journals/jamanetworkopen/fullarticle/2802556.

3. Ryan Mackman, "How ER Overutilization Hurts Healthcare," Salient Healthcare, August 7, 2019, https://www.linkedin.com/pulse/how-er-overutilization-hurts-healthcare-ryan-t-mackman-mba-mha.

4. Cesar M. Jaramillo, "Reducing Low-Acuity Preventable Emergency Room Visits by Utilizing Urgent Care Center Services via Mobile Health Unit Diversion Program," *The Journal of Urgent Care Medicine*, Vol. 16, no. 6 (March 2022), https://www.jucm.com/reducing-low-acuity-preventable-emergency-room-visits-by-utilizing-urgent-care-center-services-via-mobile-health-unit-diversion-program/.

5. Jaramillo.

6. Sax, *Evaluation of the Emergency Severity Index*.

7. D.T. Stephenson and J.R. Price, "Medically Unexplained Physical Symptoms in Emergency Medicine," *Emergency Medicine Journal*, Vol. 23, no. 8 (August 2006), https://www.ncbi.nlm.nih.gov/pmc/articles/PMC2564157/.

Chapter Ten
The Doctor Will See You Now . . .
and Any Other Time You Want

1. "What is Mounjaro? And Does It Work Better for Weight Loss than Ozempic and Wegovy?" UC Health, May 15, 2023, https://www.uchealth.org/today/what-is-mounjaro-and-how-does-it-work-for-weight-loss/.

2. Sara Gottesman, "Patient Autonomy in Direct Primary Care," *Academic Commons*, Columbia University Libraries (2022), https://academiccommons.columbia.edu/doi/10.7916/5e1v-fb97.

3. Grand View Research Report, "U.S. Concierge Medicine Market Size & Trends Report, 2030," https://www.grandviewresearch.com/industry-analysis/us-concierge-medicine-market-report.

4. Association of American Medical Colleges, "AAMC Reports a Mounting Physician Shortage," June 11, 2021, https://www.aamc.org/news/press-releases/aamc-report-reinforces-mounting-physician-shortage.

5. Grand View Research Report, "U.S. Concierge Medicine Market."

Chapter Eleven
I Want That Test, Too!

1. Alex Janin, "Wealthy People are Getting Full-Body Scans. Early Detection or Unnecessary?" *The Wall Street Journal*, August 24, 2023, https://www.msn.com/en-us/health/medical/

wealthy-people-are-getting-full-body-scans-early-detection-or-unnecessary/ar-AA1fK6hr.

2. Christina Koch, Katherine Roberts, Christopher Petruccelli, and Daniel J. Morgan, "The Frequency of Unnecessary Testing in Hospitalized Patients," *American Journal of Medicine*, Vol. 131, no. 5 (May 2018; published online December 7, 2017), https://www.ncbi.nlm.nih.gov/pmc/articles/PMC8628817.

3. Centers for Disease Control and Prevention, Division of Laboratory Systems (DLS), "Strengthening Clinical Laboratories," (2023), https://www.cdc.gov/csels/dls/strengthening-clinical-labs.html.

4. Fariss Samarrai, "Health System Works to Reduce Unnecessary Testing, Promote High-Value Care," *University of Virginia News*, July 29, 2019, https://news.virginia.edu/content/health-system-works-reduce-unnecessary-testing-promote-high-value-care.

5. The Commonwealth Fund, "U.S. Health Care from a Global Perspective," January 31, 2023, https://www.commonwealthfund.org/publications/issue-briefs/2023/jan/us-health-care-global-perspective-2022 .

6. Khang T. Vuong, "How Much Do Lab Tests Cost Without Insurance in 2023?" Mira, March 2, 2023, https://www.talktomira.com/post/how-much-do-lab-test-cost-without-insurance.

7. David Robson, "Hypochondriacs: Why it's Not Always Just in the Mind," *BBC Future*, February 15, 2022, https://www.bbc.com/future/article/20220215-why-even-just-testing-for-diseases-can-make-us-feel-ill.

8. Paul Sawers, "Daniel Ek's Neko Health Raises $65M for Preventative Healthcare through Full-Body Scans," *TechCrunch*, July 5, 2023, https://techcrunch.com/2023/07/05/daniel-eks-neko-health-raises-65m-for-preventative-healthcare-through-full-body-scans.

Chapter Twelve
Horses, Hay, and Hypochondria

(no notes)

Chapter Thirteen
Wearing My Health on My Sleeve

1. Jerusalem Post, "MIT Researchers Design Bra that Detects Early Stages of Breast Cancer," *Jerusalem Post*, July 29, 2023, https://www.jpost.com/science/article-752965.
2. University of California, "Engineers Develop the First Fully Integrated Wearable Ultrasound System for Deep-Tissue Monitoring," *SciTech Daily*, May 27, 2023, https://scitech-daily.com/engineers-develop-the-first-fully-integrated-wear-able-ultrasound-system-for-deep-tissue-monitoring.
3. Lu Tian, Ji Shourui, Jin Weiqiu, et al., "Biocompatible and Long-Term Monitoring Strategies of Wearable, Ingestible and Implantable Biosensors: Reform the Next Generation Healthcare," *Sensors*, Vol. 23, no. 6 (March 2023), https://www.mdpi.com/1424-8220/23/6/2991.
4. Bob Curley, "What Cancer Experts Think About New Wearable Monitoring Devices," *Healthline*, September 16, 2022,

https://www.healthline.com/health-news/researchers-de-veloping-wearable-device-to-measure-cancer-tumors-be-neath-the-skin.

5. Curley.

Chapter Fourteen
Living with Uncertainty

1. Mohammad Almalki, Ibrahim Al-Tawayjri, Ahmed Al-Anazi, et al., "A Recommendation for the Management of Illness Anxiety Disorder Patients Abusing the Health Care System, *Case Reports in Psychiatry,* Vol. 2016 (May 2016), https://www.hindawi.com/journals/crips/2016/6073598/.

2. All quotes in this paragraph are from Naomi A. Fineberg, Luca Pellegrini, Aaron Clarke, et al., "Meta-Analysis of Cognitive Behaviour Therapy and Selective Serotonin Reuptake Inhibitors for the Treatment of Hypochondriasis: Implications for Trial Design," *Comprehensive Psychiatry*, Vol. 118 (2022), https://www.sciencedirect.com/science/article/pii/S0010440X22000402.

3. Akemi Furuyashiki, Keiji Tabuchi, Kensuke Norikoshi, et al., "A Comparative Study of the Physiological and Psychological Effects of Forest Bathing (Shinrin-yoku) on Working Age People with and without Depressive Tendencies," *Environmental Health and Preventive Medicine*, Vol. 24, no. 1 (June 2019), https://www.ncbi.nlm.nih.gov/pmc/articles/PMC6589172/.

4. Mathew P. White, Ian Alcock, James Grellier, et al., "Spending at Least 120 Minutes a Week in Nature Is Associated with

Good Health and Wellbeing," *Scientific Reports* 9 (2019), https://www.nature.com/articles/s41598-019-44097-3.

5. Susan Abookire, "Can Forest Therapy Enhance Health and Well-Being?" *Harvard Health Publishing*, May 29, 2020, https://www.health.harvard.edu/blog/can-forest-therapy-enhance-health-and-well-being-2020052919948.

Chapter Fifteen
Solutions to Improve Our Country's Health

1. Dan Farber, "Steve Jobs Thought Different," CBS News, October 5, 2011, https://www.cbsnews.com/news/steve-jobs-thought-different/.

Closing Thoughts
Marnie's Take on the Man Who Cried Wolf

(no notes)